The Form of Things

By A. C. Grayling

The Refutation of Scepticism
Berkeley: the Central Arguments
The Long March to the Fourth of June (as Li Xiao Jun)
Russell
China: a Literary Companion (with S. Whitfield)
Moral Values
An Introduction to Philosophical Logic
Wittgenstein
Philosophy: A Guide Through the Subject
Philosophy: Further Through the Subject
The Quarrel of the Age: the Life and Times of William Hazlitt
The Meaning of Things
Herrick: Lyrics of Love and Desire
The Reason of Things
What is Good?
The Heart of Things
Descartes
Among the Dead Cities

The Form of Things

of Things

Essays on Life, Ideas and Liberty
in the Twenty-first Century

A. C. Grayling

Weidenfeld & Nicolson
LONDON

First published in Great Britain in 2006
by Weidenfeld & Nicolson

1 3 5 7 9 10 8 6 4 2

A CIP catalogue record for this book
is available from the British Library.

ISBN-13   978 0 297 85167 7
ISBN-10   0 297 85167 5

Typeset by Input Data Services Ltd, Frome

Printed in Great Britain by Clays Ltd, St Ives plc

Weidenfeld & Nicolson

The Orion Publishing Group Ltd
Orion House
5 Upper Saint Martin's Lane
London, WC2H 9EA

The Orion Publishing Group's policy is to use papers
that are natural, renewable and recyclable products and made
from wood grown in sustainable forests. The logging and
manufacturing processes are expected to conform to the
environmental regulations of the country of origin.

www.orionbooks.co.uk

Contents

Rights and Liberties

Acknowledgements

Many of these pieces appeared first in the *New Statesman*, the *Independent on Sunday*, the *Literary Review*, *The Times*, the *Financial Times*, *Index*, and elsewhere; I am grateful to the editors of these journals for the opportunity to air these ideas in their pages, and as always to Catherine Clarke, Alan Samson and Naomi Goulder for their various and continuous helps.

Preface

'And because they were philosophers and seekers after the beauty
that underlies the form of things, they made the picture express
its own significance, and every song find echo in the souls of
those that heard.'

L. A. CRANMER BYNG, *A Lute of Jade*

A human life might be a brief thing, in comparison with the long roll of history, and the even longer span of universal time in which history itself is a mere drop. Yet a human life is also a diverse thing, full of possibilities; for people live many lives in one, sometimes without realising it, because they have different biographies in the different worlds of imagination, experience and hope they occupy.

At their best, such lives retain their diversity while centring on an integrating point that makes sense of all that belongs to it, rendering those various worlds concentric and allowing the lessons and amenities of each to inform the others. Recognising what one realm of experience can teach another is something of an art, though luckily nature often takes a hand too, and helps make the hoary head wise at last. But as Francis Bacon taught in his *Wisdom of the Ancients*, commenting on the tale of the Golden Apples of Hippomenes, art can outstrip nature, by 'art' here meaning philosophy, the continuous 'preparation for life' that helps to make life rich and good, or – when otherwise – courageous and noble.

To draw together the threads of one's various experience,

one does well to look for where the threads' ends touch and intertwine in the multiplicity of the world. That, in turn, involves being alert and observant; it involves reading, thinking, conversing, learning, enjoying, judging, being sceptical, being open-minded – in short, it involves electing oneself a votary of the 'considered life'.

The essays constituting this volume, highly miscellaneous in character, are modest contributions to that task from one point of view. They are about very various ideas and topics; some are polemical, others more reflective; they come at aspects of things from widely different angles. What unifies them is that they all provoked a response in one and the same person wishing to understand the world better, and to enter the fellowship of conversation about it therefore.

Miscellanies have a distinguished history in the literary and philosophical tradition. Herodotus is the first great miscellanist, and from him through Pliny, Plutarch and Aulus Gellius to Montaigne and Bacon, Addison and Steele, Dr Johnson, Lamb and Hazlitt, De Quincy, R. L. Stevenson, Augustine Birrell and Hilaire Belloc, the tradition is strong. The premise for them all was that essaying contributions to the great conversation was like offering pieces for a mosaic that would in sum depict something true about the human condition, and how it should be endured or if possible enjoyed – but at least understood. And if the pieces were luminously coloured, or of clear glass, so much the better.

Each essay here is self-standing. This is the fifth in a series of essay miscellanies – all sharing the same hope of offering something to the conversation humankind has with itself about what matters – but it does not depend on the earlier collections in any way, and is as self-standing as the individual essays in it. Still, it is worth remarking that, as with many of the essays in those earlier collections, the form of the essays here is delib-erate; and that remark applies not least to the very short ones,

which are aimed at hinting and suggesting merely, as prompts –
something it is worth mentioning to those who forget that 'wit',
of which brevity is the soul, is more than humour, but includes
witness, and what is witting rather than unwitting, and once
meant intelligence, and even knowledge; 'Ye shall abide with
me till that I wit what ye are,' says the queen to the fair knight
in Malory's *Le Morte d'Arthur*, giving the word its original
sense; and with brevity too.

The final section contains longer polemical pieces occasioned
by political threats to the civil liberties once cherished in the
homeland of the Anglophone world. I have left them in their
original state as a witness to a time of regression, in the hope
that others later will see how reluctant some of us were to yield
the liberties so hard won by our forebears.

REFLECTIONS

REFLECTIONS

Aiming for the good

Just as all roads lead to Rome, so all subjects lead to the same set of questions about the fundamentals of human experience. Each in its own way casts light on those questions, and illuminates the many dimensions of what it is to be human, and how to live a good life.

The famous first sentence of *Anna Karenina* says that all happy families are happy in the same way, and all unhappy families are unhappy in their own particular way. Tolstoy is comprehensively wrong about that: all unhappy families are unhappy in exactly the same way, while all happy families are so because they have achieved their own way of living positively together. Their members have found the unique arrangement of compromises, of mutual understanding, of allowing one another space, and of being generous to one another, which ensures the happiness of each and therefore the happiness of the whole.

Still, Tolstoy's mistaken claim, in provoking this reaction, suggests an interesting thought about how one can try to be a flourishing and achieving individual, and thus a happy one; for the reaction teaches that there are many different ways available to people to find their route to a flourishing life. One of them – an important one – is philosophical reflection; for the following reason.

Grief and loneliness, depression, despair and failure – those things (usually in combination) are the human lot at least at times in all our lives. Moreover, we all know that to have the most treasured things in life is to risk their loss – for a central example: to love somebody is to bargain for losing that person ultimately, by death or the other chances that bring major change. It is a cliché, but no less true for being one, that there are always going to be bruises. The life in which there are no difficulties and pain is an extremely rare one, and probably has that character because the person living it is insufficiently reflective or sensitive – which means that it not only lacks the lows but the highs as well.

Still: the obvious but key point is that we are all going to be lonely at times, and depressed, and faced with the terrible experience of grief and loss; and we are all from time to time going to fail.

And this is where philosophy becomes important: not as sticking plaster or aspirin reached for after the event, but as a preparation for life. Some popularisers of philosophy give the impression that philosophy is a kind of medicated bandage for life's cuts and bruises, but they thereby do both philosophy and life a disservice. Philosophy is far more accurately conceived of as a form of prophylaxis, part of the anticipation of living, involving thought in advance about how one would try to brace oneself in grief, or how one would try to cling to ideals and principles, beliefs and hopes, even when one is profoundly depressed, or faced with failure. These are the times where intellectual and moral courage are required. If, when griefs are accumulating, one manages to cling to the belief that the best things in human life are still deeply valuable and worth pursuing, that is what it is to be morally courageous.

The noblest kind of life is the courageous life. It is easier to live such a life if one is prepared and has a strategy. The point about being philosophical in the true sense of thinking, reflecting, seeking to understand and to tolerate, and trying to inform oneself, is therefore that it provides a strategy, a framework, for living well.

A part of that strategy, of course, is to remain flexible. As Maynard Keynes used to say, 'When the facts change I change my mind. What do you do?'

One good way of formulating a strategy is to think of life as a narrative of which one is oneself the author, the maker of the story of one's life; putting some shape to it, having goals and aims, and adhering to chosen ideals or principles that inform one's outlook. Sartre once famously said that one should not live as a character in a novel because true narratives have beginnings, middles and ends, and therefore one is presupposing the end – in the sense of the termination of life, making one in effect live like a dead person. But Sartre's view is wrong. To live for ends means living for goals, not termination.

Another cliché that encodes a profundity is that one should live as if this day were one's last, and also as if one is going to live forever. This latter idea has recurred in philosophy often. The very word 'recurrence' reminds one of Nietzsche, whose injunction was to 'live your life as if you were going to repeat it eternally'. The advice, in short, is to try to make life the very best kind one can live, so that repeating it eternally will not be hell.

And that at last raises the key question, 'What then is the best kind of life?' The philosophers all have their suggestions. Aristotle said that the very best life is the life of contemplation. It is a life of meditation upon the very highest and best thing there is, which is thought. So it is the life of thought thinking about itself. That does not on the face of it seem so compelling a view; but it becomes more so if one translates it into a suggestion about the life of the mind, of intellectual endeavours and the pursuit of knowledge. But even this would not be for every taste.

Epicurus said that we must pursue pleasure and avoid pain. He also said, 'All things in moderation, including moderation.' His idea of pleasure was not far from Aristotle's: a somewhat ascetic ideal of intellectual life. His idea of pain, or at least the seeds of pain, was exactly what modern Epicureans think is a good time, involving the fleshly pleasures.

Plato said that the point of life is 'the struggle to achieve the good'. He had an elaborate metaphysical conception of what 'the good' is as the highest absolute form of ideal. Unfortunately he never tells us quite what 'the good' is, save that it is achieved by finding balance, harmony and proportion in character and action – ideas that apply not only to the flourishing individual but to the good society.

In my view 'the good' is something we are all familiar with: acts of kindness, affection, the enjoyment and instruction derived from art and literature, the pleasure afforded by natural beauty – all these are aspects of the good, worth seeking and having. The good is the heart of things ('A turn, and we stand at the heart of things,' Browning wrote); it is present to us in our daily lives all the time. The search for the good is made to seem long and arduous, but that is not the case. One achieves a degree of philosophical understanding – of preparation for life that is being lived now – at every moment: each day is itself an opportunity for preparation, even as it is lived. Everything one does – visiting a garden, reading a novel, going to the cinema, listening to a concert or a lecture – is another contribution to an understanding of the good and of being prepared for life each day. None of these things is by nature arduous, nor do they take a great amount of study. It just takes openness and receptivity, and a preparedness to reflect and to hear.

It is quite hard sometimes to hear things. We make ourselves deaf and blind by means of our unrecognised prejudices and assumptions. We acquire such rooted ways of thinking about the world, such natural prejudices, natural blindfolds and ear-plugs, bad mental habits ('it is failure in life to form habits,' Pater remarked), that we too often do not see and hear things we ought to if we are to get the rounded picture. So the idea of being open and receptive has to be taken seriously. For one key thing: it is hard to listen to other people's points of view in a world where other points of view can sometimes be dangerous. Where conflicts between points of view can result in war and terrorism, where the natural reaction is to retire into one's own traditions and ways of thinking, the overall tendency is to close minds, to narrow them down, to make everyone more conservative.

And yet these challenges are invitations to be more thoughtful and open, not less; more considering about things in the hope that not only will one's own life continue to grow richly and flourishingly, but also so that we can take into account the important fact that it is not possible to be truly happy and fulfilled if other people are known to you not to be those things. Edmund Burke remarked that although there is very little most of us can individually do about the world's problems, this fact is not an excuse for doing nothing at all.

Consider the hypothesis (which anyway is overwhelmingly likely to be true) that the universe exists as a result of the play of natural laws alone. Late in the billions of years that the universe has existed, in one little corner of it, consciousness flickers into existence and over some millions of years grows into self-awareness, and for some thousands of years more produces art, painting, philosophy, science, literature and music. It produces moments of great happiness and also great suffering, great kindness and love, and great cruelty. And then – because of a virus, or a collision with another planet, or because the aware beings are so stupid that they blow ourselves up – consciousness comes to an end and the universe reverts to being a neutral play of blind natural forces.

Now imagine that the sum total of good that emerged from the relatively brief existence of consciousness in the universe's history outweighed the sum total of bad. That fact would make the whole history of the universe a good thing. But imagine if the sum total of evil outweighs the sum total of good. That would make the whole history of the universe a bad thing.

This suggests a striking thought: that if we desire that the sum of good should outweigh the bad in the universe's history, we each have a responsibility to make the universe a better place by increasing in it the sum of good. And there is no better place to start than with oneself and one's local habitat in however small a way.

The beautiful and the good

A s a result of the quarrel between those who think beauty is an objective thing, capable of being measured and scientifically explained, and those who think it is a subjective thing, the product of changing tastes and historical accident, a whole library of theories with polysyllabic names ending in 'Ism' has arisen, to delight pedants (so many nits to pick, so many distinctions to draw) and to confuse those who otherwise know what they like (as the phrase goes) when they see it – plain honest folk for whom objectivism, subjectivism, emotionalism, essentialism, formalism, expressionism, instrumentalism, modernism, representationalism, etc., are the sounds of a distant battle, full of sound and fury, signifying nothing.

Only: it does not signify nothing. Aesthetics – for such is the battle's name, denoting discussion of the nature of beauty and art – signifies humanity at some of its best. Contrast the sounds of this battle with those of a real one – guns, bombs, screaming aircraft, screaming people – and ask which you prefer. If you instead ask, 'Which is more representative of humankind?' the answer has alas to be: both. But surprisingly, it is the battle of aesthetics rather than the battle of guns which is on the majority side of human avocations. That might seem a large, if not downright false, claim, given the fact that no year is known to history in which some group of humans did not rise up to smite some other group. But it is easy to see that the peaceful and constructive things humans do far outweigh the terrible things they do.

Proof: look at the cities of Europe. They took centuries to build. They contain theatres and libraries, bookshops and galleries, sewage systems and paved roads, schools, post offices, hospitals, homes with furniture and comforts for the great majority. None of this took a day or a week to make; it took centuries of civilisation and culture. And this means that it took centuries of co-operation, agreement, discussion, forethought and stability. Europe abounds in cities; not even the tonnages of high explosives and incendiaries that rained down on them during the 1940s interrupted them for long, despite the terror and ruin caused.

Is that not amazing, and hopeful? Amazing that the concrete works of peace are so stubbornly durable, while those of war are by contrast so temporary and futile; so that in the long view of history the worst excesses of human destructiveness – atom bombs, even – are erased and healed over, if not in half a generation then in two; and the works of peace resume.

The Greeks thought that the perfect human body, male or female, was as much an ethical as an aesthetic symbol. They meant that its proportion and harmony, its life and health, if replicated in the sphere of mind, would – in its conjunction with the physical – constitute a perfect human being. In this way aesthetics contributes powerfully to the idea of 'the good' – the good life, the good society. There is of course no such thing in reality as a perfect human being, or a completely good life, or a wholly good society. But as the success of peace over war shows, it obviously helps to have the ideal.

Beauty

Beauty is an effect, an impression or impact, on the human imagination. People and things are accounted beautiful when they provoke a distinctive mixture of yearning, admiration and pleasure in a beholder, drawing the beholder's eyes and thoughts irresistibly to them, prompting a need to contemplate them longer, and even to possess them. When people encounter things with this power they call them beautiful rather than merely charming or attractive, to mark how impossible it is to be indifferent to the hint of majesty and mystery that are part of beauty's essence.

It is said that female beauty is the most powerful drug in the world, capturing the attention and will of men and other women alike. That makes it more than mere prettiness, which can pall after a time. Beauty is also independent of any formulae about symmetry or geometry, fashion or style. Despite the fact that there can be differences of opinion about beauty, it is not an entirely subjective matter. There is something about the human emotions that places limits on competing possibilities of what can and cannot count as beautiful; the proof of which is that finding something beautiful can make us weep, or fill us with desire. No doubt these are facts about how the human brain is constructed; but just as with what seems funny or sad, pleasing or repulsive, the range of human responses is wide even though they are partly biological, because experience and conditioning have their part in the picture too.

Different societies at different times have chosen contrasting things to focus upon in celebrating beauty, but the differences are largely superficial. Consider the statuary of the ancient Greeks, the 'gopis' who sport with Krishna in Indian art, the faces of Fra Angelico in the fifteenth century, the nudes of Ingres in the nineteenth century; all these, from across time and the world, are readily judged beautiful now, despite the disparity of context and value. Biological necessity is enough by itself to make the configuration of a young woman beautiful to most men, just as certain shades of colour are more attractive to the human eye, and certain harmonies of sound to the ear. All this reinforces the point about how often judgements of beauty agree.

Love makes the beloved seem beautiful, no matter what. Stendhal called this 'crystallisation', to suggest the idea of concealing something plain or ugly with a beautifying layer of glitter. He took the idea from a Salzburg tradition, in which youths and maidens dangled little twigs down the salt-mines until they were covered in salt-crystals, to give each other as gifts of love. But the beloved's beauty is an entirely subjective thing; the fact that only one person can see it says more about the nature of love than of beauty itself.

'There is no excellent beauty,' said Francis Bacon, 'that hath not some strangeness in the proportion.' That is why beauty escapes definition, except in the immediate response of the heart and eye.

I do not especially like ranking things, given that there are so many different kinds of beauty and achievement in the world, not least because it is hard to compare natural beauty (as in landscapes, human faces and the sound of the sea) with man-made beauty (as in dance, painting and music). And that leaves aside the strange high beauty to be found in science, philosophy and, above all, mathematics.

But to choose an example of beauty which expresses the best of human desire to make something lovely for the amelioration of ordinary life, I would pick Song dynasty monochrome porcelains, and for preference the plain ones, that is, those without incised patterns or illustrations, and the 'crackled' ware, with their fragile abstract traceries. The extraordinary hue and depth of the colours achieved by Song potters is better seen than described, as is the purity of their glazes. The best examples are pieces from the famous Ruzhou kiln, which produced solely for the Imperial court. There are only sixty Ru porcelains surviving, in exquisite shades of powder blue, turquoise and aquamarine, with very fine crackle glazes and weightless slender shapes.

I choose these because, after living in China for a time and visiting it regularly for many years thereafter, I came to think of porcelains as expressing the best of China's very ancient and remarkably rich culture. Seeing the exquisite Song pieces in the Imperial Palace collection in Taibei capped matters: there is only one thing in the arena of human craft that compares with the beauty of those breathtaking objects, and that is music.

Colour

At the height of the Victorian Age the colour of health was white: white bread, white flour, white sugar – for white was the signature of everything refined and pure, which is why it became the colour of the bridal gown, token of the unsullied virginity being publicly and quite often willingly sacrificed on the altar of the newly invented romantic version of matrimony.

Today the colour of health is brown – brown bread, brown flour, brown rice: the unrefined, natural, organic whole grain is the symbol of heartiness and therefore (of course) happiness. What was once the peasant's leavings – husks, chaff and fibre – is now the cognoscenti's repast of choice.

But the brown ideal tripped up in one respect: the suntan. White skin was once the acme (if no acne marred) of beauty. The snowy breast and cream complexion were accounted perfect, for among other things they contrasted with the sunburned, windburned, rain-hardened skin of the field labourer, tanned to leather.

In the 1920s playboys and playgirls discovered that the French Riviera was cheap and empty in the summer, for it was traditionally a wintering place, whose mild climate offered escape to denizens of cold northern Europe. The playmates' advent made the Riviera a fashionable summer playground, and with it the sun-bronzed body.

The gods, as we know to our cost, do not like us to have fun. Our enjoyment of refined white bread and rice led to bowel cancer. Our enjoyment of sunbathing led to skin cancer. Who knows what medical disturbances, waiting to be discovered, lurk in the brownness of the whole grain, or what deficits of blood and marrow, liver and brain, bide their time in those who loiter palely indoors when the sun blazes outdoors, deprived of skin-fed vitamin D.

In China, white is the colour of mourning, brown is the colour of drought. Chairman Mao's revolution took place under the Red Flag; his wisdom was immortalised in the Little Red Book. The future, he announced, was Red. Consistency suggested to him the inappropriateness of the fact that a red traffic light means stop, so he ordered a reversal in the arrangements. After several weeks of mayhem on China's crowded city streets, with traffic both going and stopping on both colours, and pedestrians dying under the resulting wreckage, the original arrangement was reinstated.

When Europe languished under the ownership of kings, only royalty was allowed to wear purple and only nobility was allowed to wear crimson. Anyone who wore the wrong colour was punished, sometimes severely. In colonial and post-colonial times, skin colour determined an individual's place: pink at the top, black at the bottom. Thus every colour bears a meaning, from the blush on the cheek to the bloom on the peach, and little has changed since time began.

It is odd to think that birds and butterflies see colours humans cannot see, though the latter think they rule the world.

Dance

At almost any exhibition of contemporary art the thought that crosses one's mind is: Is this rubbish, or am I missing the point? One could take the view that most of it is indeed rubbish, but of a useful kind: for it takes a lot of compost to make a flower – and flower lovers live in hope. Cynics say that the problem is the existence of art colleges, where people spend their time gluing cereal boxes to bicycle tyres (conceptual art), or demand that people watch them doing it (performance art), but at least they serve a great purpose in establishing the contrast between art in Andy Warhol's sense ('art is what you can get away with') and the art of dance, which is real art, and where there is little possibility of faking it.

Contemporary dance is in fact *the* cutting-edge art form of our time. Even before there can be questions of choreography, design, staging and performance, there has to be such a high level of fundamental skill available – and of the most unequivocal kind – that the mere raw material of dance is itself a thing of art. Then add the fact that the twentieth century, and increasingly its second half, saw a majestic efflorescence of choreographic talent in both the classical and modern arenas, and the case is made.

Dance can be narrative or absolute, and although it is hard not to make it beautiful, it can sometimes achieve that feat. Even then it retains its power to cast spells. The basic formula is simple: dance is about human bodies creating shapes and lines in space, and in chosen ways changing the relations between them over time, usually as an interpretation of music, or in partnership with music, or at least a beat. The paradigm of dance is rhythmic movement using conscious patterns of steps and gestures, and in ways that are expressive and typically (though sometimes deliberately not) graceful. That makes dance four-dimensional at least, although when one adds the emotional dimension – most often, the response to such traits of beauty as grace and youth, for dance is the business of perfected human physicality too – one sees why it is not enough to think of dance as mere movement.

The usual, though not invariable, sixth dimension is music, often as powerful as the dance itself; and the seventh dimension, important when dance is performed for an audience, is design – costume, setting – ranging from a naked stage (and dancers) to elaborate palaces and mountain glades, exotic fabrics, and dramatic lighting. As performance for an audience, dance is theatre that needs the least but can profit from the most that theatrical science offers.

Dance is probably the oldest of all art forms, along with song. Pictures on pottery shards nearly 10,000 years old show dancers in action. It comes naturally: following a rhythm, imitating the regularities in step or hand-clapping of others, moving to a pattern in hoeing or cutting, swaying to a beat, is something integral to human physiology. In what used to be called 'traditional' societies, any excuse to dance, and any means – a patch of clear ground and a hollowed log for someone to beat a rhythm on – is enough to get the whole community going, from infants to the aged. In those societies everyone dances from infancy to old age; in ours, we mainly do it in the two decades between the onset of adolescence and the end of courting. After that, self-consciousness sets in.

But that only applies to us as performers. As admirers of the various gifts that human beings can display, we delight in athleticism, musicality, acting skill, beauty of form, graceful deportment, and we might go to see them on the sports field, in the concert hall, the theatre, or the art gallery. But all these combine in ballet and modern dance. Dance is therefore a summation of what we most like when we watch others. Sitting at a pavement café observing passers-by is a pleasurable entertainment; attending to the simulacra of other lives in soap operas is a gripping entertainment; watching dance includes and transcends them both.

A distinctive fact about the world cities New York and London is that they are rich in dance. In the course of almost any year in them one can see the work of such giants of choreography as Kenneth Macmillan, Frederick Ashton and George Balanchine, and in modern dance the genius of some at least of Anthony Tudor, Twyla Tharp, Pina Bausch, Jiri Kilian, Mark Morris, William Forsythe and others.

My own introduction to dance occurred early, as an expatriate child in central Africa seeing whole villages of Africans dance bare-footed on hard ground, their stamping, swaying, ululating unison a hypnotising vision. Once established, the symmetry of that style of dance begins to invite complexity – syncopated steps, changing patterns, counterpoint, subtle over-rhythms, enabling the dance to evolve beyond communal enjoyment of semi-trance into the realms of narrative: hunting the leopard, marrying the chief's daughter.

When I first saw ballet on the Covent Garden stage, also when young, I recognised that the basic elements of dance were still present, but wonderfully transformed by the sophisticated language of the form to enable it to tell complex stories, and to explore the emotions that give them their point. The formal vocabulary of ballet, like structures of metre and rhyme in poetry, is the framework on which the art is built. In modern dance that framework is stretched, bent, looped, buckled and abandoned at need, to go into different fields of expressiveness – as an alternative to, not as an advance beyond, the classical forms, which the work of Ashton, Macmillan and others shows to be inexhaustible.

Ballet and modern dance can only leave you cold if you start with prejudices about them. Laddish distrust of boys in tights, or a pose of disdain for high culture as the preserve of the rich and affected, are the typical barriers. But hardly anyone who sees ballet and modern dance without preconceptions – who realises that what they enjoy about dance in music videos is here by the truck-load and more – can fail to be a convert. It is, after all, the most natural and most enchanting of all entertainments, the easiest to enjoy. And it is true art: there is, to repeat, no faking it.

Funerals

Death is a favourite topic among Romantics (note the capital), who are apt to mope about the countryside declaiming verses, usually their own, on the subject of how one unkind look from the beloved will consign them to an early grave. Observers have been known to pray for the unkind look to follow forthwith. But death as a conceit – really, as a metaphor for revenge: for what the Romantics convey, in their iambics, is a threat to punish their beloveds for unkind looks – is as remote from the sad necessities of the real thing as Timbuktu from Ultima Thule.

On the morning of the day on which this was written I attended a funeral. It was an unusual one, in being a requiem Mass in Latin, chosen in advance by the deceased as her preferred manner of sending off because she was both an emotional and superstitious believer, for whom Latin is the deity's language, and the bells and smells of the Tridentine mass the only proper accompaniment to its use. Most of the congregation were treated to what was assuredly the habitual experience of medieval peasants: not understanding a word of what was going on, and in ragged lack of uniformity, standing, sitting and kneeling (and sometimes all three at once) as bidden by ambiguous hand-signals from the altar.

The spectacle of grown men performing the ritual of the mass would normally be enough to numb philosophical reflection, but as this was a requiem mass, thoughts naturally turned to the solemnity of death, and the way it is treated in our life-affirming age. Societies in which alcohol is seen as the proper fuel for transporting the dead into the new phases of their existence – as, first, a larger presence in the hearts of those who loved them, then as personal memory, then as family history, and at last as a statistic – have great advantages over those that merely serve tea and monosyllables.

I have seen funerals in Africa, where people truly know how to mourn, helped by professional wailers, and in China, where the bereaved dress in white like brides and set off firecrackers to keep demons away. As an amateur anthropologist from another world, pondering on the inner experience of those who, by the order of things as spouse, parent or child, are most affected, one notices that what is obvious there is obvious everywhere: first, that whatever its form, a funeral is an absolute parting, and the more clearly that hard fact is seen, the sooner heals the wound it makes; and second, that the prompt for mourning is universal, however individual cultures understand it: for although not all call it love or need, the grief feels just the same.

Hate

Paradoxical as it may seem to say so, love is more prevalent in the world than hate. This is because love takes many forms, and is felt by individuals for many more individuals than those they actually hate by name. True, many people hate many others in the mass, as racism and xenophobia show; but this occurs usually without such haters knowing any one among the hated well enough to justify the sentiment. They hate in the abstract, in a generalised and stereotyping way; which in practical terms is the same as hating just one other person – the one that the hater meets and mistreats in the street.

The great William Hazlitt wrote an essay called 'On the Pleasure of Hating' in which among other things he argued that hate is necessary as a foil to love, like the dark cloud that sets off the rainbow, and that moreover it answers a need in the human breast for something to stir it into action and feeling: for pure good grows insipid, and even love cools over time, he says, whereas hatred alone is immortal.

Hatred is the emotion felt when a certain complex of fear, ignorance and antipathy overflow a limit, combine themselves into a single thick glomerate, and begin to master the thought-processes of their owner. This does not guarantee action, but it too often results in action. When it does it can be extremely dangerous: its logical conclusion is murder, even mass murder, as demonstrated by the Holocaust.

There is (inevitably) a website that monitors expressions of hatred. It is called Hatewatch. At the time of writing it reported

(1) the growth of white supremacist racist music in America as a result of promotion by a label called Panzerfaust Records, (2) the angry protests of parishioners and parents over a Californian school's decision to enrol a gay couple's children, and (3) the activities of anti-immigration farmers calling themselves 'Minutemen', who volunteer to patrol the Texas–Mexico border to keep 'illegals' out of the US. Note how, in all three, the same fundamental ingredients exist: ignorance, prejudice, mean-mindedness, callousness, lack of imagination and self-righteousness. Some mixture.

Hermann Hesse said, 'If you hate a person you hate something in him that is part of yourself.' So what does this say about white supremacists, anti-gay protesters and self-styled 'Minutemen'? The ugly emotions that flow through the sewers of hatred, if they are in truth an everted expression of self-loathing, suggest a very profound warp in the hater's soul. But that would be true anyway, since it is not easy to hate without being hateful oneself, whether or not only others see and feel the fact.

If there is one certainty in the case, it is, as La Rochefoucauld observed, that hating puts people below the level of those they hate. The racist, the xenophobe, the anti-gay protester and the religious fanatic bent on killing the infidel, are each accordingly a morally reduced form of human. Beware hating them, therefore, because that is to sink low indeed.

Hedonism

Human history has been weighed down with ordinances of denial from those who claim to know what the gods want of us – which seems mainly to be that we should not enjoy ourselves, even though they have given us natures attuned to pleasure. Whatever the agency that brought about mankind, it furnished the ear for harmony, the nose for scent, the mouth and tongue for savours ... and so on all the way down and back up again, to that greatest organ of pleasure: the brain, which can fly, dream, sport with Amaryllis in the shade, and conquer the world – all in a moment.

Not all humans are fools, we may be thankful to note, and recognising the fraudulence of the promise that wholesale denial will be posthumously rewarded, we can turn to philosophy instead. Epicurus taught that the best life consists in pursuit of pleasure and avoidance of pain, which only seems feckless until we understand that for him pleasure meant talking with friends in a garden, taking water when thirsty and bread when hungry, whereas the festivities of bed and board seemed to him merely the harbingers of pain: hangovers, pregnancies, obesity, illness, disgust and death. 'All things in moderation,' he counselled; even moderation itself – for the Epicureans occasionally let their hair down, in order to remind themselves that true pleasure has its roots in sobriety.

Epicurus's view is one species of 'hedonism'. As a general theory of what is morally best for humankind, hedonism teaches that the pleasure of others as well as one's own is the right goal to pursue. 'Psychological hedonism' is a quite different animal; it is an empirical theory claiming that people only ever seek their own pleasure, and if they promote that of others it is only as an instrument to their own. This view seems plausible at first glance, but two moments' reflection reveal the mistake. We all genuinely desire the pleasure of others at times, and the fact that we take pleasure in their pleasure does not detract from the desire's benevolence.

But the important thing about hedonism is that it is a moral theory, that is, a theory about what we ought to strive for. It is a theory about the good, and in particular the good life. It says that the highest value is pleasure, including the pleasure of others. And this second clause rules out taking pleasure in harm to others, but instead enjoins an attitude of moral respect: for only if we pay attention to the interests of others can we be sure to act in ways that add to their good as well as to our own. This is why Oscar Wilde rejected the so-called Golden Rule, 'do unto others', for it makes you take yourself as the standard of what everyone wants, whereas what you should instead do is to see and respect others' differences, and act accordingly.

Unfashionableness

Where do fashions come from? They come from what is unfashionable – or at least, from what was fashionable long enough ago for it to have ceased being unfashionable. It has been well said that a style of dress ten years ahead of its time is thought of as indecent, a year after its time as grotesque, and a century after its time as beautiful. The interstices of this rhythm explain the way fashions oscillate, pulsing in and out of focus as on a psychedelic screen.

From time to time some of the people who lead the way in fashion choose instead to lead the way in Unfashionableness – only thereby to create a new fashion. There is no paradox in this; it is as logical, psychological and anthropological as can be. The true dictators of fashion are those with the confidence to be different; the true followers of fashion are those with the lack of confidence that makes them want to be the same as those who are different. And so it goes.

In the great age of Chinese civilisation, the Tang Dynasty (AD 619–907), women wore dresses with deep décolletage, diaphanous figure-hugging shapes with skirts flowing enough to delight a Herrick, and high waists as in our own Regency times. In the succeeding Song Dynasty (AD 960–1276) women were obliged to cover up again, and the horrific practice of foot-binding began. The moral character of an age is as clearly stamped on its sartorial fashions as a ruler's head on a coin. Fashion is, so to speak, the outward and visible sign of ethics; which is why the moralisers of the world get so exercised over the degree of visibility of ankles and thighs, breasts and buttocks.

And hair. In all the 'Religions of the Book' God is held to dislike hair, at least in church or synagogue. That is what you might call a top-down moral theory; if the hair has to be covered, so does all the rest.

Although the word 'fashion' mainly suggests the excesses of the catwalk in women's clothing, it applies of course to everything, from literary forms to motor cars, from medical practices to political nostrums. The novel has been in fashion mainly since the nineteenth century, prior to which it was regarded as a mildly vicious form of distraction apt to keep young ladies from their duties, or (worse) to put ideas into their heads. For too large a slice of the twentieth century, and still today in America, male circumcision was a fashion. ('Slice' is here the *mot juste*.) In the politics of contemporary Western polities, the fashion is for democracy.

All these will change, and almost all back to something tried in the past, and by definition rejected or superseded. Take democracy: it seems unthinkable that any Western countries might renege on it as the most sacred of sacred cows, but it has happened within living memory, and there can be no guarantees that it will not happen again. Indeed, if the nature of fashion is anything to go by, it will.

Montreux

From the late nineteenth century until the start of Hitler's war, Montreux and its neighbours on the Swiss Riviera were a honeypot for the rich and famous. Grand palace hotels rose on the north-eastern shore of Lake Geneva, commanding views of stupendous beauty across the quiet water to the Alps. Each day English aristocrats, Russian princes, New York financiers, maharajahs, stars of opera and theatre – the scions of wealth, privilege and fame – strolled on the lake shore, or through the vineyards on the hills behind them, or yachted on the lake. By night they congregated in magnificent Art Nouveau and neo-Baroque ballrooms for fancy-dress parties and concerts, dining in black tie and dancing away the night.

Anyone of an old-fashioned turn of mind – leaving privilege, riches and fancy-dress balls quite aside – might enjoy resurrecting that kind of holiday: sitting on a balcony in a handsome, high-ceilinged old hotel with good room service, looking up from the pages of a book across a lake to mountains massed on its further shore, and drinking in the fresh bright air that flows from both. It seems unkind to the Vaudois economy, and impeachably exclusive, to say that one could be glad that mass tourism prefers seasides.

The lake shore of the Vaud quivers with literary and musical history. Here Stravinsky wrote *Petrouchka* in 1911 and *Le Sacre du Printemps* in 1912. Richard Strauss spent his winter months at the Montreux Palace Hotel and in 1947 there wrote 'Im Abendrot', the first of his 'Four Last Songs'. After writing *Lolita*

Vladimir Nabokov took up residence in the Cygne Wing of the Montreux Palace Hotel and passed the last sixteen years of his life there, dying in 1977. Thomas Mann's *Magic Mountain* was filmed in the same hotel.

All this says nothing of the jazz and television festivals which supply Montreux's current fame; but none of it might have happened were it not for Rousseau first, and Byron after him. Rousseau lived at Vevey, and wrote *The New Eloise* there, with its fabulous love-story of Julie and Saint-Preux, and its shockingly Romantic conclusion in which the dying Julie repudiates the reason of the Enlightenment for the passion of the heart.

Julie caught her death of pneumonia in the waters round the Château de Chillon, one of the world's most spectacular castles. In its dungeons languished Bonivard, the hero of Byron's 'The Prisoner of Chillon'. Byron scratched his name on the pillar where Bonivard was chained by a Duke of Savoy as punishment for his defence of Geneva's liberty. The poet's iconic signature can still be seen, helpfully framed by the current chatelaines.

In tribute to Rousseau the great English essayist Hazlitt spent a happy summer at Vevey, gazing at the Alps rising wave after wave above Evian across the water, and receding as they rose into a dreamlike distance. From Sarah Bernhardt to Stravinsky, from David Niven to Mikhail Gorbachev, he has had any number of famous successors since. Apart from its festivals, Montreux is quieter now and has slipped considerably down-market; a McDonald's occupies prime place on the main water-front, providing fuel for the skateboarders who clatter about nearby. But along the Quai des Fleurs in the direction of Chillon memories of former splendour remain, and nothing can efface the tranquil majesty of the lake and the soaring peaks around it.

A fast train, keeping such exact time that one can set one's watch by it, connects Geneva to this enchanted corner. It flashes through vineyards, sunflower fields and neat villages, the view from its windows confirming the stereotype of Switzerland as ordered and unflurried. But it is a country uncomfortably poised in historical terms. It had a bad press recently for its banking of Nazi treasure and its belated reparations to members of Europe's Jewish dispossessed. The amend-making is indirectly related to Switzerland's slow but inevitable shift towards membership of the European Union.

A Swiss doctor friend claimed, in the face of my incredulity, that in the mid-1990s Switzerland had one of the highest rates of HIV infection per capita in the world. Was this, I asked, because of the heroin addicts of Zurich? He said no, it was because Swiss business travellers, released from the repressions and restrictions of home, made such good use of Bangkok brothels and New York bath-houses in the '70s. Among other things, this alleged fact suggests that the Swiss are painfully conscious that others see them as buttoned-up and over-hygienic in their emotions. Does the caricature stem from the German-speaking parts of Switzerland? The French-speaking parts have the elegance and savoir-vivre of the French everywhere. Anyway, the claim to high HIV rates seemed an odd way to dynamite the myth.

All this seems far from the pleasant lakeside path of the Quai des Fleurs, alongside which the small boats curtsy at their moorings, and above which the villas and apartment blocks look out over tree-filled gardens at the Alps. But then, this walk to the romantic Château de Chillon seems far from everything except the highest beauties of nature combined with the tenderest amenities of civilisation, which has surely always been the chief attraction of any town capable of being what Montreux was in its heyday.

The death of civilisations

W hat brought about the end of societies such as those that built Great Zimbabwe, Angkor Wat, the imposing Mayan temples, and the majestic statues of Easter Island? Each of these societies lasted for many centuries, and invested vast resources in their material culture; yet each vanished, leaving behind them little more than haunting remains of lost greatness.

In his *Collapse: How Societies Choose to Fail or Survive,* Jared Diamond argues that collapsed societies are far more than a romantic mystery. They are an intellectual problem, and moreover one that has urgent relevance for today, because the evidence tells us, he argues, that each is the result of environmental problems identical to those we now face.

The problems in question are formidable: deforestation, diminishing rain forests, over-fishing, soil erosion and salinisation, climate change, pressure on water supplies, depletion of energy sources, pollution and population increase, especially in regions where all these other problems are most acute. To make his case that just such difficulties were responsible for the demise of past societies, Diamond explores in detail two examples of environmental problems – the Bitterroot Valley in present-day Montana, and Greenland of the Viking era – and several others at less length: Easter Island and its south-east Polynesian neighbours, the Anasazi culture of the south-western United States, and the Maya civilisation. Contemporary Rwanda, Haiti, China and Australia come under Diamond's eye too, and after them he considers the global situation, the effect of big business on the world environment, and the remedies currently on offer for the problems thus created. He believes that we have a chance to save the planet if we will attend carefully to past experience. His account is crammed with considerations drawn from ecology, history and anthropology.

But: did Diamond choose evidence suited to his case, and fail to consider alternative examples of social decline and failure? Consider the Egyptian, Persian, Roman, Byzantine, Mughal, Ottoman, Chinese and British empires, all once great, rich and flourishing, now all vanished as empires (though the Chinese empire is reviving fast), and in the first five cases leaving magnificent ruins behind them. They seem to invite far more complicated stories, in which environmental problems play little part, if any. One cannot say that deforestation or water shortages precipitated the fall of the Byzantine or British empires. The ruins of the Roman Forum are no less dramatic than those of Angkor Wat, but cannot be attributed to soil erosion. Those of the Upper and Lower Nile are not related to any change in that river's behaviour between five and two thousand years ago. Is Diamond stretching a point in implying that environmental problems (and especially deforestation, which occupies a key position in most of the stories he chooses to tell) is the pivotal reason in social collapse – *all* social collapse?

For the examples Diamond chooses, though, the argument he advances is compelling and in most cases conclusive. Easter Island definitely once had forests, and is now bare of trees, and likewise with the Anasazi's Chaco Valley. Deforestation devastates the local weather, water supply and soil quality of pre-industrial societies, and deprives them of fuel for cooking, warmth and tool-making. The connection between deforestation and social demise in such cases is clear. And since what is common to all the cases Diamond adduces is that people ran out of things to eat – this after all is the bottom line of what environmental degradation does: it makes the sources of food (whether land for planting, fish for catching, deer for hunting, and so on) incapable of supporting the population in question – he has to be right.

And although that applies only to the societies he chooses to examine – societies whose well-being was very sensitive to changes in their environment – what he says is far from irrelevant to contemporary advanced societies, which might be even more vulnerable than Easter Islanders or Rwandans to environmental difficulties, especially because advanced contemporary life makes such punitively damaging demands on nature.

Diamond lists five factors in society-destroying environmental collapse: failure to understand and to prevent causes of environmental damage; climate change; depredations by hostile neighbours; the inability of friendly neighbours to continue trade; and finally, how the society itself deals with the problems raised by the first four factors – a common failing being the dislocation between the short-term interests of elites and the longer-term interest of the societies they dominate: a telling point.

By far the most significant factor is of course the first one, so Diamond concentrates on it most. His interest in Easter Island, in particular, is prompted by the fact that it manifests the effects of all five factors paradigmatically, which makes it serve as a metaphor for the present: planet earth is today's Easter Island.

But not all is doom. In fact Diamond ends on an upbeat note: there is hope, because we have the lessons of the past to learn from, and not only the negative lessons of collapsed societies but the positive ones of those that have found solutions and flourished – Japan, Tonga, Tikopea, Inuit Greenland, the Dutch in their polders. Their successes have an added support today, says Diamond: the upside of globalisation, which is information exchange.

Still, what about the more complex lessons of the decline and fall of great empires that do not fit the environmental model? If it turned out that their examples are more important for understanding ourselves today, we would have made a serious mistake indeed by looking in one direction only, however important in its own right. One suspects that great empires collapsed for political rather than ecological reasons, and while they lasted were able to sustain themselves as long as they did because their broad environmental bases – their geographical spread – protected them from difficulties that destroyed smaller more localised communities. If this is right, then the internationalist, globalist project of protecting humanity against its own exploitations of nature is the right way to go, an idea that runs against the contemporary current of nationalism and regionalisation.

What this suggests, at the very least, is that there can be no substitute for study of the lessons taught by history and politics, even in the age of ecology.

Time

An average human life (so it is tempting to point out at every opportunity) is less than a thousand months long. One third of those months are spent asleep, so a conscious human existence averages about six hundred months merely. A lifetime is thus a truly fleeting thing, lodged between a sleep and a forgetting; and there scarcely seems time to draw breath in it, before its last breath is drawn.

The first mystery of time, then, is how little of it anyone has. The second is how unimaginably vast time seems on either side of the mere moments humans manage to occupy. If the universe's history were compressed into an hour, the time that humankind has existed would barely fit into the last fractions of a split second of that hour. If humanity succeeds in extinguishing itself through ecological disaster or nuclear war, the spark of intelligent life that flared in this corner of the cosmos would be scarcely noticeable between the massive weights of time that stretched before and after it.

Is it possible to explain time? St Augustine put his finger on the nub of the difficulty when he said, 'If you tell me to meet you at such-and-such a time, I have no problem; but if you ask me what time is, I cannot answer.' As a bishop St Augustine should not, of course, have worried about time, which in theology is a minor matter, for the reason that the deity is eternal, and 'eternal' means 'outside time'; and since the deity and his eternal realm constitute ultimate reality, it follows that time is unreal. And one should not worry about what does not exist.

Voyaging

A ccording to an Arab proverb, a human soul can only travel as fast as a camel can trot. This explains jet-lag. Boeings full of human bodies might be hurled from one continent to the next, in defiance not just of oceans and mountains but of time itself, and of the ancient pre-lapsarian rhythms of the primate physique; but the inner human essence cannot be so cavalierly treated, and it follows at the only pace it can.

To travel steadily, therefore, you had best walk. Since in our urgent age this is impractical – no one would get far, in any sense of this phrase, by foot alone – a bicycle is a good compromise, if not ridden too fast. Better still is a horse; it is good company. Here too, though, limitations enter. Bike and beast can serve only the parochial aspect of travel. One's needs might be local most of the time, but neither a bicycle nor a horse is going to get one from Paris to Moscow, from Dublin to Los Angeles, in time for much business worth doing; so alternatives are necessary.

The answer, obviously, is to go by train when land intervenes, and by ship otherwise. Truly, unless one has experienced long days of travel by either means, living through the transitions of climate and ethos they make possible, one has not travelled at all: one has only been flung about. In the days before air travel people regularly had time to adjust themselves to parting from one place and preparing themselves for the next, in the meanwhile having a physical and moral holiday. It is scarcely surprising that few have a sense of proportion nowadays: they end before they have begun, they arrive before they have left, they oscillate among ambiguities of time and place, belonging to neither.

It is well said, '*experto crede*'. I have travelled for days on end, and sometimes weeks, by train across Africa, India and the Far East, by ship in the China Seas, the Pacific and the Atlantic, and by foot through most of the world's greatest cities from Toronto to Tokyo. Compared with the vertiginous bustle of a flight to and from Zurich in the same day, or the red-eye from New York, the chance to gather one's wits and sense one's passage over the vast curve of the earth, inching along and registering details as they pass, is exquisite. Rapidity is a blur; only think of the contrast between roaring off the runway at Heathrow, and pulling from the dockside on the Huangpu river in Shanghai, and nosing among the chaos of junks and tramp steamers out towards the slow brown breadth of the Yangtse river, and thence into the East China Sea – flat as glass in calm weather, home to typhoons otherwise.

It takes six hours to go from western Europe to the east coast of America by aeroplane, six days by ship. But the six flying hours have to be deducted from life's total, whereas the six sailing days are automatically added. No contest, I'd say.

Wah-Wah

B ecause India was the jewel in Britain's imperial crown, and because India captured and governed the British imagination more thoroughly than the British did either to India, other stretches of the perpetually sunbathed empire occupy less of our national memory. This is especially true of that other forgotten region of imperial heat and dust, Africa; and the reason is that such places as South Africa, Rhodesia and Kenya were true colonies, many of whose white residents had gone there to make permanently new lives, not to be temporary expatriate officials.

But there were little Indias in Africa, in the sense that the expatriates running them on London's behalf were quite clear where 'home' was, and almost all planned to retire to Surrey or Hertfordshire when the time came. Nyasaland in East Africa, where I was brought up, was one; a time-frozen slice of Edwardian England surviving fifty years after the Edwardian Age had ended, in which most of the worst of England was distilled to a purity of toxicity hard to imagine now. Yes, it had its delights – the beauty of the place, for one thing, and the pleasures of the exploitative lifestyle, for another; but at its worst it was a claustrophobic, introverted, over-heated cantonment of pettiness and snobbery, with life revolving around the country club, itself sussurating with whispered gossip and malice, and where bridge, alcoholism and adultery were the chief of the few available diversions.

This world is captured with pitch-perfect precision in

Richard E. Grant's film *Wah-Wah*. Its setting is Swaziland in south-east Africa – another of the mini-quasi-Indias – and if one looks for a moment beyond the film's painful and poignant central story, one sees a vivid portrait of the life of British expats in sub-Saharan Africa in the quarter-century after 1945. Every representative type is there, and Grant documents the friction-filled, inescapable, inexorable social life of the small community they form with eye-watering truth. It made me, the former expat who writes these words, feel as if he had been transported by djinns right back to the heart of the nightmare.

Even the view from the main characters' house in the film – a beautiful and breathtaking expanse of Africa seen from a hill, with the obligatory swimming-pool in the foreground was practically identical to the vista from my family's veranda, for our house was also built on a hill, for the cooler air and fewer mosquitoes, with in our case a panorama towards Mozambique across the lip of the Great African Rift Valley and the inland sea of Lake Nyasa.

In Grant's film the native servants are marginal players: just so were they in the eyes of their imperial masters back then. They padded about in their uniforms, serving tea and emptying ashtrays, scarcely regarded, hovering inconsequentially on the periphery of the expatriate vision. In Grant's film the intensely internal network of relationships among the expats themselves absorbs all the available energy and oxygen of human possibility; just so were those relationships in reality. Grant has reproduced that world – now completely vanished and, as time advances, leaching from the memory of its survivors – with unblinking documentary fidelity.

Grant's film, by the way, is outstanding for many more reasons than just this documentary realism about an almost-forgotten corner of British imperial history. But it is its fidelity in this respect that will strike the few survivors of that time most, and it is worth their bearing witness to the fact that Grant got it absolutely right, so that the future will know it too.

Language purity, language change

Mystery and controversy are directly proportional: the less we know about something, the more we argue over it. Language is a prime example. It is the supreme characteristic of human beings, sharply distinguishing us from other animals by virtue of the powers of reasoning and social organisation it provides. Yet the origins of language are shrouded in obscurity, and so is its nature. Philosophers still struggle to explain how meaning attaches to the signs we use in communicating with each other, and psychophysiologists still labour to understand the basis of linguistic capacity in the brain. Much has been learned about these matters in recent times, but that much is a speck compared with the mountains of ignorance that remain.

The bafflement of experts has never inhibited public discussion of one particular hot potato, viz. language change. A familiar and acerbic quarrel rumbles between purists and liberals, the former deprecating what they see as falling standards, the latter maintaining that language change is natural and unexceptionable. This latter view confers an imprimatur of respectability on split infinitives, terminal prepositions and other features of linguistic usage uncongenial to purists.

Speculation about the origins of language was never widespread in religious ages, rendered uneccessary by the assumption that language was God-given (and, in one tradition,

God-confounded into many tongues as a punishment for presumption). But from the sceptical eighteenth-century Enlightenment onwards the question has been alive, to such an extent indeed that august academies for a time banned discussion of it, as a fruitless because impossible enquiry, a breeding ground for absurd speculations – such as the theory that the world's original language was Chinese (the reason: that those descendants of Noah who went east after the Flood had avoided Babel), or the theory that early humans acquired language by imitating parrots.

In recent decades there has been a vigorous revival of enquiry into language origins. Researchers hope to make progress by pooling evidence from animal ethology, archaeology, psychology, evolutionary biology, anatomy and linguistics itself – including comparative study of those recently emerged or emerging languages called pidgins and creoles.

This formidable array of science looks promising, but the promise is far from fulfilment. To date, the mountain's labour has produced only a mouse, in the form of mere guesswork and some surprisingly poor reasoning.

Did language begin simply and become complex, or did it begin messily and then neaten? Did it emerge rapidly at a particular moment in human evolution, or slowly over aeons? The answers depend on prior answers. What is the point of language? Is it for the communication of facts, or for 'social grooming' and bonding? And does the answer to this tell us whether language is a social artefact or a biological (genetic, 'hard-wired') capacity? The evidence seems to suggest that languages simplify as they age, losing such complexities as cases and genders and compensating for any resulting losses of precision by making word-order crucial to sense. Sanskrit, ancient Greek and Latin are related languages, in that order of descending complexity. Chinese, a language with a long continuous history, has shed almost all noun and verb endings marking case, person and number. Can the implication really be that the first languages were even more grammatically and syntactically complex than Sanskrit? Given that we suppose verbal communication to have begun with grunts and cries – or, as some have hypothesised, in chanting and singing – how could this be?

Students of language do indeed summon the aid of current views about human evolution. These tell an 'Out of Africa' story, in which a group of apes was corralled in the harsh dry eastern portion of Africa by the formation of the Great Rift Valley. Their cousins in the lushly forested west had an easier life and therefore evolved into chimpanzees and gorillas; but the EastEnders, to survive, had both to stand up and smarten up. On the basis of this hypothesis – itself as fragile as the little pile of bones it is based on – the claim is that somewhere about there and somewhere about then (the vagueness is irreducible: we have no H. G. Wells time machine that would take us back to check), language *might* have begun; suddenly or slowly, in gestures, lip-smacks, or both – no one knows.

'Might' and 'possibly', 'could have' and 'presumably' dog the pages of any account about *origins*. But as scholars progress through the *evolution* of language (that is, the development of grammar) and its spread and variation, caution diminishes. One reason for this greater note of confidence is the empirical evidence provided by pidgins (pidgins are rudimentary languages developed as a convenience of communication between speakers of different languages) and creoles (pidgins that have become the first languages of children knowing nothing else). In Tok Pisin ('talk pidgin', i.e. 'pidgin talk') the sentence 'lukaut: planti switpela kaikai i save bagarapim tit hariap' means 'look out: lots of sweet food will ruin [your] teeth quickly'. Say the words and the meaning becomes amusingly clear.

Does an examination of Tok Pisin illuminate the general story of linguistic evolution? Surely there are reasons for doubt. One might argue that pidgins and creoles do not clarify that story because they do not recapitulate that process. They are, instead, examples of a quite different process, one that can only begin from an already evolved language. For pidgins are corruptions – in the sense of simplifying adaptations – of existing languages. They provide evidence of degenerative change in existing languages under certain pressures, not of linguistic evolution in the first place.

And perhaps, in the very notable poverty of their expressive capacity, pidgins should trouble those who take the liberal view of language change. Liberals, remember, do not mind the disappearance of distinctions and the simplification of grammatical forms, even those that mark logical differences. This tendency is what, in the extreme, produces pidgins: simple clumsy languages incapable of nuance, detail, abstraction and precision. For this, a pidgin has to become a creole, and then begin the evolutionary ascent again to greater expressive power. It might be that the fullest realisation of the latter only occurs when the creole yields a literature.

The moral anyone should draw from speculations about linguistic origins and evolution, namely, that language change is natural and inevitable, should therefore not obscure what is at stake in this other debate. For, as the example of pidgin shows, not all change is benign.

Let it be agreed that language *change* is natural and inevitable. This unexceptionable fact does not entail that we can, still less should, be unreflective about language *use*. Consider an example. A few years ago certain reductions in London bus services were explained in notices which, in hopes of spreading good cheer nevertheless, concluded: 'So, the buses will run smoother, with less delays.' In its context this sentence is perfectly clear. But it is a logical farrago, for the point concerned the smooth running not of the *buses* but of the bus *services*. For accuracy of the legal, philosophical and literary kinds, therefore, the comparative adverb 'more smoothly' is required in place of the comparative adjective 'smoother', and the elided noun 'services' is needed, yielding 'the bus services will run more smoothly'. And in the same spirit, since 'delays' is a count noun, not a mass term, 'fewer' is required in place of 'less'. Why *required* in these exacter cases? Because they avoid the chief threat to language's communicative capacity, viz. ambiguity. Suppose the Bus Supremo had said to his minions: 'Make the buses run smoother!' In this form of pidgin, his minions would be hard pressed to know whether he had suspension springs or timed services in mind.

In one way, language change is not what it seems. Spoken forms of languages change all the time in unstable ways – think of the very different colloquial versions of English that have, with some rapidity, succeeded one another on the streets of London over the centuries. The written form of the language changes more slowly and regularly, and educated speech moves with it. An eloquent 'Estuary English' speaker of today – 'pu' a bi' o' bu'er on va bread I give yer' – would barely understand the street slang spoken in London during the Napoleonic Wars; and a cockney then would not easily have followed his ancestor of Orange William's day. Yet because there is a more stably evolving educated discourse, we read Dryden and Hazlitt with ease, and could as easily converse with Locke and Coleridge were they to rise from the dead.

Part of the reason for this is that a mature language is one that carries its history with it, chiefly in its literature; and careful users of the language are loath to lose the increments in expressive power that its evolution bequeaths. A service is therefore performed by those who 'care about clarity and precision, who detest fuzziness of expression that reveals sloppiness or laziness of thought', as the language maven William Safire put it, and who therefore give language change 'a shove in the direction of freshness and precision ... to preserve [its] clarity and colour'. This is not conservatism, because it recognises and accepts that language changes. Rather, it is the view that such change need not always be at the expense of expressive power, for we are not the helpless victims of change, but can influence it.

These are considerations we will better understand when we understand more about the evolution of language – a goal still far off, although perhaps not as exceedingly remote as the goal of understanding language's origins.

Questions of language

In its closing decades the conscience of the Austro-Hungarian Empire was kept by one man, the rebarbative and formidable Karl Kraus, owner of the magazine *The Torch*. In a famous editorial Kraus remarked that one can infer a person's moral character from his prose style. This is surely false – many wicked people have written like angels – but it suggests a related truth· that the character of a person's mind can be judged from his use of language. This is because language is the chief instrument of thought, and when it is employed accurately, flexibly and powerfully, it enhances the thought it expresses.

It matters therefore that one should think constantly about one's use of language, and keep it in verbal trim, much as an athlete trains his body. Reading is the key, together with reflection on what one reads, and a lively curiosity about the language's possibilities. Unfortunately, too many people read little, reflect less, and have no curiosity about their native tongue. Even readers tend to be lazy about consulting dictionaries – most indeed fail in the duty to own a good one.

Not only should every home have a good standard dictionary, it should also have a book of reference about the language mainly spoken in it – which is not the same thing as a dictionary. Such a book would give a perspective on the language, a 'feel' for its genius and eccentricities. How many words does (to use the example of the language in which this is written) English contain? Should one write 'privatize' or 'privatise'? What is the origin of such expressions as 'gay', 'wally', 'loo', 'OK'? Why are the letters of the alphabet ordered as they are? Is there a difference between 'partially' and 'partly'? What is the longest English word? And even – is there a name for people who drink their own bathwater?

Each of these questions is a representative one. They are examples of the queries received by the lexicographers of the Oxford Dictionaries. In response to the barrage of enquiries they receive, these patient and knowledgeable folk decided in 1983 to set up the Oxford Word and Language Service – appropriately, OWLS – and subsequently published a distillation of their work in book form: *Questions of English* (edited by Jeremy Marshal and Fred Macdonald).

One of this book's chief virtues is its non-prescriptive way of advising on language use. Language is a protean beast, ever growing and adapting. It cannot be restrained by purists or Academicians – though they can and rightly should endeavour to maintain its expressive powers and accuracy – for a language that does not change is dead. In so various and geographically widespread a language as English there can hardly even be rules. Accordingly, the owls of OWLS are open-minded and sensible. Should one say 'the majority of people are' or 'the majority of people is'? The latter, say the owls, is strictly right, but the former is well established in practice, and therefore acceptable. 'Castor suger' or 'caster sugar'? Both are right. 'Do you eat soup or drink it?' Either. And so on.

But the owls are not fence-sitters. They explain origins and derivations, they explain why some of us hate the split infinitive; they distinguish and define. And from time to time they say: 'here is a misconception' or 'it would be more logical to say ...' and they always make great good sense.

And now for an answer to some of those questions. There is no word in use for a person who drinks his own bathwater (although a few ripe terms spring readily enough to mind), so the owls, who know their Greek, offer one: 'autoloutrophilist'.

The longest word in English is, as one would expect, a medical term: pneumonoultramicroscopicsilicovolcanoconiosis, forty-five letters (and eleven letters longer than its nearest rival), meaning a lung disease of the silicosis variety.

And the number of words in English? Well, this is trickier: it depends how you count them. The complete Oxford English Dictionary has about a quarter of a million full entries, about twenty per cent of which are for words now obsolete. But this takes no account of multi-word compounds, phrases, certain kinds of technical terms, scientific Latin names, and – most importantly – the multiple senses of a single word. Counting these latter, English possesses about three-quarters of a million words, about 100,000 of them obsolete.

To make sense of these numbers one needs to know that an educated person would be expected to have an active vocabulary of about 30,000 words.

To read the *Sun* newspaper you require a vocabulary of about 800 words; which is the standard minimum for getting by in most natural languages.

Long life

I n youth we feel immortal, but our first grey hairs bring home the unpalatable truth. We age from puberty onwards, paying the price of our reproductive capacity – such as it is: for humans are among the least fertile of species, and science dismayingly informs us that human infertility is worsening. And although people in the West now live longer than ever before, it is not because the limits of age have been pushed back, but because we have conquered diseases that once struck early in life, such as smallpox and tuberculosis.

With its sometimes uncomfortable capacity for accuracy, the science of ageing points out that our grey hairs are in fact white. We may have suspected as much, but whereas a touch of grey at the temples bespeaks the prime of life, white hair denotes senility: so we have stuck with the euphemism. But euphemisms do not defeat truth, they merely obscure it. Most of us wish to live long, but we do not wish to grow old. Throughout history quacks have profited from our hunger for prolonged youth, or at least healthy longevity. Has science brought this grail closer?

The answer, as we might expect, is both yes and no. On the one hand we have learned that there is nothing inevitable about ageing. Neither the timetables of life, nor its upper limits, are fixed anywhere in the biological realm. Experiment has shown that the average lifespans of many different creatures can be hugely extended, and not in tottering dotage but in health and vigour. Different creatures have travelled by different experimental routes to this result. Some have been saved by celibacy, others by eating low-calorie diets, yet others by being bred from old parents. In humans the effects of ageing can in some cases be dramatically reversed, as when hormone replacement therapy makes it possible for post-menopausal women to bear children.

On the other hand, the mechanisms of ageing are so complex that, so far, they remain a mystery. What has been learned from experiments on fruit flies and mice might teach us little about human ageing – and therefore, as the joke has it, anorexic continence might only make it seem as if you are living for ever; in fact it is as likely to kill you sooner.

There are however definite links between sex and death. The male marsupial mouse of Australia kills itself by its promiscuity, mating ceaselessly and without stopping to eat or drink, until it falls dead from exhaustion in the very act. This is an extreme example; but it demonstrates an interesting fact. Very high levels of stress are recorded in this little creature during its suicidal rut. Stress prompts the adrenal glands to produce corticosteroids, and prolonged production of steroids causes problems. Bones become fragile, muscles waste, diabetes develops, the body bloats with salt and water, skin thins, hair falls out, the immune system weakens in its battles against cancer, infection and parasites. These unhappy symptoms are characteristic of ageing. Stress and ageing, it would therefore seem, are two sides of the same coin.

The link seems to be that procreation and health make competing demands. It is as if evolution prompts creatures to invest more in reproducing themselves than in living long. The body is a disposable husk for our DNA; youth and vigour ensure the transmission of our genes, and when the season of procreation has passed, the body clocks run down. It is the organs of generation that reach senescence first.

Somewhere in this fact lies the elusive answer to the question of how ageing might be arrested. One suggestions is that hormones are the key. This idea is championed by Roger Gosden, a professor of reproductive science who was one of the first to promote the cause of hormone replacement therapy for menopausal women, and became famous for his work, stopped by public outcry, in helping infertile couples by transplanting eggs from dead foetuses into living ovaries. Gosden points out that lowered hormone levels result in less muscle and more fat of the unhealthy male type, and in reduced bone mass and metabolic rate. Treatment with oestrogen, testosterone, growth hormone and melatonin show definite benefits. Gosden cites, as a case in point, the health bonus brought by the female contraceptive pill: it has reduced heavy periods, anaemia, benign breast lumps, and uterine and ovarian cancer. And it might have brought these benefits by restoring a lost natural order of lower ovulation rates, of the kind common in the past when women were either pregnant or breast-feeding for much of their maturity.

Gosden is sure that there will be a 'cure' for ageing one day, arising from better understanding of genes and hormones; but it is just as well that this is still some way off, because we need time to consider what the world will be like when the majority of its human inhabitants are centenarians. We are already, given that most of us now live to the normal life limit, as concerned about *how* we die as *when* we die, which is why debates about euthanasia have become increasingly important. When life-spans can be extended, perhaps indefinitely, what further deep dilemmas will swim into view?

Sympathy

It was widely agreed among participants in the revived debate over the foundations of ethics in eighteenth-century Europe that it is a condition of the moral life, and of the existence of community, that moral agents – human beings – should be capable of sympathy. Chief among those who argued in this way are David Hume, Adam Smith and Edmund Burke. They differ from each other in the exact nature of their theory of moral psychology, and in particular in their accounts of sympathy. But there is a large measure of agreement among them concerning its role.

It seems unexceptionable to argue that sympathy has a foundational role in ethics. Hume and the others assumed that a capacity for sympathy is in some sense innate – in what sense need not detain us, for there are unproblematic ways of making a case for the innateness of many capacities – and there is much in favour of agreeing. We can allow that it is not universal; some theories of criminal psychology suggest that there are people who more or less completely lack the kind of imagination and sensitivity on which sympathy depends. But unless a capacity for sympathy were widespread it would be very hard to see how moral life is possible, for we would not understand how agents lacking it could appropriately grasp how matters stand with another, and – an important further step – make that understanding a basis for acting in ways adjusted to the needs, desires or interests of that other. This is the key to sympathy as a condition for morality, whatever finer-grained account one might give of it.

The aim here is to assume the correctness of this claim, and to take up a problem which then appears. It is clear that, left to itself, the sympathy for which most of us have a natural capacity tends to be parochial. We put those close to us before those remoter from us, and we often fail in our sympathies across barriers of inexperience, as when, for example, one who has never suffered bereavement sees less into another's grief than one who has.

This indeed is a chief cause of the human predicament. Resources are limited, whether naturally or artificially; and so are sympathies. Competition arises, and with it, unless there are means of resolving it, conflict. The need for customs and laws, but above all for ethics as the shaper of attitudes and actions, is therefore pressing. The failure of these resources for overcoming the conflicts which wrack human existence, at all scales from the personal to the international, is to blame for that predicament.

If there is a general tendency for sympathies to be parochial, to be limited by the finitary characteristics of human life, the question arises: by what means can they be extended? Can one hope that they might be extended further and generally, in the hope that the moral community will not always labour under the constraints generated by limitations of parochialism, but aspire to some higher level of civilised behaviour?

This question is related to the famous one asked of Socrates by Meno: 'Is virtue teachable?' It is not the same question, but it is allied because it asks whether there is a way of educating the sympathies, thereby enhancing prospects in the moral realm.

There is an affirmative answer. It is to say that by encouraging exposure to *narrative art* – the novel, drama, film – the sympathies can be educated, refined and enlarged.

The suggestion is not as simple as it seems. It requires hedging with caveats, of which two must be mentioned directly. The first is that this of course is not proposed as the only way this can be done, although arguably it is the most powerful. The second is that there is no suggestion here that questions about the ways moral sensibility can be refined have to proceed in tandem with acceptance of a particular set of values as the one which the process must promote. On the contrary, the proposal is largely formal; it aims at generalising about aspects of moral psychology in ways that do not depend on accepting this or that particular ethical outlook. But they assume some values, a limited number of relatively uncontroversial ones, and they assume that in almost any dispensation some disvalues would be widely recognised as such, and can therefore be used as a constraint by settling what insight into, and concern for, others had better not result in.

What, then, is the relation of culture and aesthetics – especially, narrative arts of the novel and drama – to ethical life? It is taken to be a commonplace that acquaintance with literature and the arts heightens insight into the human condition, and promotes the human sympathies which many moral philosophers from Hume and Burke onwards have claimed to be necessary for morality. To what extent, and in what way, is this true?

The argument of these philosophers proceeds as follows. A person will choose to act in ways which recognise, and are sensitive to, the interests of others, only if he is able to grasp how things are for them, and to understand why those things matter to them; and, further, recognises that things being that way for them makes a claim on his concern in practical ways.

To gain access to another's perspective on life demands a certain kind of informed and interpretative sympathy. Most people can learn something about the needs and interests of others from their own experience and from their observation of people around them; but if this were the only resource, the scope of an individual's sympathies would be rather limited. Exposure to the narrative arts overcomes that limitation: they greatly widen one's perceptions of human experience, and enable one – vicariously, or as a fly-on-the-wall witness – to see into lives, conditions and experiences which one might never encounter in practice. This enlarging of the sympathies is a basis for richer moral experience and a more refined capacity for moral response.

An immediate problem with this thesis is that there were, no doubt, SS officers at Auschwitz who returned from their day's work to read Goethe and listen to Beethoven on the gramophone. Does this not destroy the link between art and the good life? Might Plato be right in arguing that art actually destroys, or at least threatens to undermine, morality? One thing the example shows is that appreciation of art is not *sufficient* for promoting moral life.

Does this refute the belief that there is a connection between art and ethics, namely, that aesthetic appreciation heightens morally relevant insight? The argument of this essay is that it does not. To see why, one has to understand the complex relationship between art and morality, education, the social order and historical thought – an understanding which throws light on each of these topics in the process.

The education of moral sensibility with regard to other-directed action is only part of the story. Socrates observed that 'the unconsidered life is not worth living'; as the point is sometimes put, 'the life of an unhappy Socrates is better than that of a happy pig'. Is this so, and if so why? The outlook here answers in the affirmative, and argues as follows. The idea of making one's own life worthwhile by choosing goals and striving towards them, deferring present satisfactions in the hope of greater rewards later, demands the imposition of a kind of *narrative structure* on one's life, as if one were the author of one's own story. Only if one has a rich array of possible narratives and goals to choose from can those choices and actions be truly informed and maximally free. Once again, exposure to stories – which in part represent possible lives – is a vital ingredient in the ethical construction of one's personal future history.

And it might be further argued that part of what makes a work of fiction, painting or theatre a work of *art* is precisely its potential to be a significant element in the interaction between narratives and lives which make certain narratives (or narrative types) immensely important to us, and life-enriching in ways closely related to the two just canvassed.

The foregoing themes, vitally important as they are, only serve as a preface to a larger debate about the nature of education and society, and the place of art and philosophy in the health of society and in making individual experience worthwhile.

It is sometimes said, erroneously, that in the Renaissance an educated person could know everything there was to be known. The remark is intended to dramatise a contrast between the exploding amount of information in our con-temporary world, and the supposedly small body of knowledge available to the best-informed person of the fifteenth century in Europe. We use the term 'Renaissance man' now to denote someone of wide knowledge; the associated negative term is 'dilettante', denoting someone who has dipped superficially into many pots of knowledge but who, for that very reason, is master of none. But 'dilettante' was once a term of praise, and the ideal of a wide acquaintance with the intellectual endeavours of mankind was seen as a good thing: in the Renaissance's 'dilettanti' were the very 'Renaissance men' we now affect to admire.

Information is not knowledge, and neither is opinion. But well-formed opinions about information come as close as anything can do to knowledge, knowledge of the kind that can be applied in practice – subject always to revision in the light of further experience.

The idea of *knowledge* presents a twofold problem. On the one hand, we lack reliable information about many crucial matters – we are for example largely ignorant about the origins of humanity and the fundamentals of human nature and mind; we know little about the origin and destiny of the universe, although we have sophisticated hypotheses about both; and we have a Babel of hotly-contested beliefs and opinions about matters of religion, morality, law and society. On the other hand we are buried under mountains of information that we scarcely have time to assimilate or organise, a situation dramatically increased in recent times by the volume of computer power available to generate, communicate and store it.

But without opportunities for reflection, information in any quantity is valueless. A synoptic view is needed, a larger picture, a review of what has been acquired and learned – and concomitantly, of the extent and nature of our ignorance. The Greeks thought of the gods as having such a perspective, looking at the affairs of men from the peak of Olympus. 'Olympian detachment' might be possible for gods if there were such beings, but from the human perspective in the midst of the fray, such a view is a lot – and perhaps too much – to ask; the best we can do is to pause and take stock.

But the kind of knowledge that makes the moral life and human communities possible, the kind that promotes sympathy and insight, is not remote from us; the very existence of the narrative arts trades on it as well as providing, by reciprocation, the increase in the reflective reader's or viewer's appreciation of what they can convey. At their best they offer genuine knowledge of the human heart, including its ugly side; and therefore the chance, at times, of an Olympian overview at least of our own lives and relationships, in which we can make sense of them, and on which basis we can make an effort to live them better.

The history of knowledge and ignorance

I magine this scene: a steep-sided lecture room filled by a crowd listening in astonishment to a young man – astonished (and in some cases thrilled) by the audacity of his lecture, the message of which swept away centuries of received wisdom and forced the audience to accept that their science had to begin again, from scratch, afresh.

The young man at the centre of this attention, despite his youth dressed in a professor's habit of gown and square cap, was Andreas Vesalius (1514–64). On the table in front of him lay a scattering of bones and an open book. The bones were those of humans and apes, the book was Galen's treatise on anatomy. Holding up the bones one by one, Vesalius proved to his audience that Galen's teachings, on which centuries of medical practice had been founded, were wrong.

What change of intellectual climate had allowed Vesalius to challenge the wisdom of antiquity? No doubt he might have done so without prompting or preparation, trusting his own genius and the results of his careful but clandestine research on exhumed skeletons. He might thereby have defied church authority, the power of academies, and centuries of tradition, unaided and without a harbinger, springing from nowhere into the light of a new intellectual dispensation.

But in fact the ground had been prepared for him, so that although his lecture on Galen was startlingly new, it had been made possible by something that had happened fifty years before, and which itself made possible the revolution in the West's conceptions of man and science. That earlier occurrence was a quiet event, at first barely noticed and thus without the brouhaha of Vesalius's lecture; but within a few years it had effected a startling new opening of minds, Vesalius's among them.

The event in question took place in a year usually celebrated for very different reasons: the *annus mirabilis* of 1492. On standard views the most significant thing to happen in 1492 was Christopher Columbus's voyage across the ocean blue, the result of which introduced Europe's imagination to undreamt possibilities. Columbus made landfall in the New World on 12 October, the same day Piero della Francesca died. A few months earlier King Ferdinand and Queen Isabella had expelled the last Muslims from Spain, and it was not long before a gush of wealth and novelty began to flow across the Atlantic into Europe through their kingdom's ports. Already, therefore, 1492 seems to mark an epoch, full of signposts to many different novel worlds.

But that same year witnessed an event that was in its way as important as Columbus's voyage or the defeat of the Moors. It was the publication of Niccolo Leoniceno's *The Errors of Pliny*. For nearly one and a half millennia Pliny's *Natural History* had been the chief repository of secular knowledge in the Western world. Leoniceno demonstrated the falsity of dozens of Pliny's statements, so causing, like a Samson of the intellect, the collapse of one of traditional wisdom's main pillars. His readers soon understood that they were faced with a world as new as the one Columbus had discovered. The ancients had been shown to be fallible; enquiry had to be begin again, to check, or rediscover – even, perhaps, to find truths entirely new.

Within twenty years of the publication of Leoniceno's book a certain Petrus Magnus produced a diatribe entitled *Everything*

Aristotle said was Wrong. It is a silly and excessive work in parts, but it amply shows how, within a generation, the mental climate had changed. Where there had once been unquestioning reverence for the masters of antiquity, there were now – sometimes – thumbed noses.

Just a few years more, and Vesalius had looked at the human skeleton for himself, instead of trusting to an ancient text on the subject. The result was *De Humani Corporis Fabrica (The Structure of the Human Body)* in 1543. On the day he announced the outcome of his research, standing in the crowded lecture theatre with a throng of professors and students looking on in amazement, Vesalius employed a simple technique: he read out Galen's description of an anatomical feature, and then held up the damning contrary evidence for all to see. The new beginning in science was empirical, independent-minded, and blunt in its challenge to other alleged sources of knowledge: the past, revelation, holy writ, the sagacity of greybeards.

Modern times had begun. With it began a new chapter in the Wars of Knowledge, whose casualties now had to suffer at the stake, on the battlefield, in the ducking-stool, and in countless other ways as the defenders of new knowledge and old fought to the death for the sovereignty of their beliefs.

The repudiation of ancient wisdom was one of the Renaissance's engines. The Renaissance was not just a rediscovery of the classical past's material culture, but of its scepticism and passion for enquiry. Demolishing the hegemony of ancient wisdom, as Leoniceno and Vesalius had done, was essential for a new beginning.

Such revolutions in ideas begin quietly but have momentous consequences. They illustrate Isaiah Berlin's remark, in the Preface to his *Four Essays on Liberty*, that thought is what changes the world. 'The philosopher sitting in his study today,' he wrote, 'can change the course of history within fifty years.'

Four principal topics have dominated the attention of humanistic enquirers throughout history: physical nature, human nature, history and how best to organise human relations in society (which is to say: ethics and politics). To give a definitive portrait of any society at any period in its history, one has to describe its contemporary views about these matters. The story of how such beliefs developed in Western societies – whether by trial and error, or by genius; sometimes in response to pressing need, but often against the hostility, not untypically dangerous, of rulers and religions – is an absorbing and exciting story.

But that story is not just a history of the growth of knowledge. It is also a story about how the growth of knowledge works as an engine of historical change and conflict. The point is a commonplace in connection with technology, especially military technology; but it is not often enough appreciated how *theories* about seemingly abstract matters such as the origins of the world, human nature, education and the basis of political rights, can result in massive historical shifts.

An example is provided by the complex of sixteenth-century events which, for brevity, is called 'the Reformation'. A large part of what drove these events was impatience with restraints on enquiry imposed by the Church. The Church taught that human reason is fallen and finite, and therefore that attempts to penetrate nature's secrets are impious. But the Reformed sensibility saw reason as a divine gift, and believed that mankind had been set a challenge by God to read the 'Great Book of the World'. There was also a school of thought in Christendom which believed that the world was given to man to expropriate at will – which meant that it was as open to the curiosity of the scientist as to the craft of the hunter or husbandman.

Another example is afforded by the medieval mystics, who claimed revelations about the nature of the universe – all of them more or less closely based upon the cosmography of Plato's *Timaeus*, one of the few works of Plato then known, and certainly the most influential. But the twelfth century re-transmission to the West from the Arab world of the works of Aristotle and the mathematicians put cosmological mysticism to flight; and thereafter the practice of spiritual cosmology vanished. Later mystics confined themselves to revelations about the nature of God and his wishes.

The defeat of spiritual epistemology is one of the chief factors that made the modern Western world possible, because it promoted confidence in human enquiry and undermined the exclusive claim to authority of supernatural sources of knowledge.

In this respect Renaissance and Reformation thought mirrored the first rise of philosophical enquiry, credited to ancient Miletus, where Thales is said to have taken the giant step of trusting to unaided human reason as a means to knowledge. By doing so he repudiated traditions of thought that relied upon beliefs about supernatural agencies to explain the origin, nature and destiny of the world.

These examples are drawn from what are conventionally labelled 'Renaissance' and 'Reformation', but in truth the story of knowledge has only just begun as the twenty-first century advances. If we can survive the fact that our technological capability lies far in advance of our political wisdom – a fact which puts us at a perilous juncture of history – we are on the brink of barely imaginable developments in which the exponential advance of technology, and imminent breakthroughs in medical science, are set to transform human experience. What will it take to negotiate this narrow bridge between our tribal past and any of the possible futures that our best reasonings can secure for us?

Actually, this question is merely shorthand for many others. One is this. From the earliest times man has invented cosmogonies (theories of how the universe began) and cosmologies (theories of the ultimate nature of the universe). They are grand theories designed to make sense of the world, its past and the laws (or powers) that govern it; and they suggest ways of influencing or even controlling it (in those earlier times, by sacrifice and prayer). In this sense religions are primitive versions of science and technology. They aspire to offer explanations: to tell us who we are, why we are here, what we must do and where we are going. The growth of contemporary science conflicts with religion thus conceived, because it offers explanations of the same phenomena in wholly different ways.

But modern science poses a problem of 'meaning': does it give us any philosophical or spiritual guidance? And it raises the additional problem of the 'unimaginable future': we are most probably only at an early point of our scientific adventure, and if we survive the incongruity between our advanced scientific possibilities and our primitive politics, we are en route for a world which we cannot now properly envisage, still less prepare for. Are there any lessons from the history of the growth of knowledge that could guide us?

Another question is this. Measurement and mathematics were among the first fruits of the need for greater social organisation in early times. They gave humanity an example of the power of reason unaided by factors external to the human mind; they were proof that the divine spark in man comes from man himself. This belief is important for the beginnings of general enquiry – philosophy in the Greek sense – which quickly led to the Socratic revolution, leading to the first humanistic enquiry into the nature, foundations and moral duties of human society. This was the moment when the history of the West changed to the course it has been following since. The internal evolution of the political-moral framework debated by the Greeks has been a tumultuous and often violent one, and it has fought (and still fights) a bitter struggle against various kinds of tyranny; but at least the nature of the battle, and what is at stake, have always been clear.

Less clear is the quiet influence of practical advances in the

life of civilisation. Hesiod and Virgil were teachers of practicalities; they wrote of agriculture and the gods. Agriculture,
architecture and engineering (including Rome's drains, high-
ways, city planning in the Empire and military technology)
all reflected the economic and political circumstances of their
times, and influenced the culture which flourished because of
them. The relation between material and intellectual culture,
and the way art and practicality interact, form a constant theme
in the life of civilisations. Practical knowledge, working quietly
in the hands of practical people, often has as great an impact, if
not greater, in shaping the history of civilisations as the genius
of individuals or the chances of fate and war. It is out of practicalities that theoretical knowledge grows. It is a commonplace
of intellectual history that Babylonians watched the stars for
purposes of divination, and Egyptians developed geometrical
techniques to redefine boundaries after the Nile's floods, and
that these techniques provided the basis for later research in
mathematics, astronomy and cosmology.

But how did these transitions in practical competency occur,
and why? What other fields of ordinary common-sense knowledge turned into philosophy and science of sufficient power to
model whole civilisations, and which did not? And when they
did, why did they?

These questions embrace, among other things, yet further
questions about beliefs concerning the body and illness, the
mind, sex, reproduction and sexual differences, eating and food,
and the relation of humans to the rest of nature. These matters
have always been profoundly significant, for all their apparent
mundanity, in the social organisation of mankind. The fine-
grained character of civilisations and their intimate histories
turn upon them.

A. J. P. Taylor wrote of the importance of railway timetables
to the origins of the First World War; equally unexpected and
even homely facts about the common culture and beliefs of

peoples have been crucial in history. Consider, for example, the difference made to the world by the demand for something as domestic as culinary spices. Courageous men ventured oceans for them, and traversed deserts; wars were fought and empires built as a result of the demand for spice in Venice and Amsterdam, in China and the East Indies. The sea routes that opened to expedite a trade that was too slow and costly across inhospitable Asia have given us much of today's politics.

At the same time, the sharp differences which these connections reveal provide another focus for understanding the relation of knowledge and civilisation. Comparisons between Western and Chinese science, medicine and technology in the period from classical times (in China, the pre-Qin) to medieval times (in China, the Tang and Song dynasties) make highly informative reading, not least because of the surprising light they shed by comparison with aspects of Western culture.

Among the tumult of themes here one must emphasise those that exemplify both the positive and negative effect of religious faith in history. Questions of hierarchy and power, literacy and knowledge, belief and fear, the violence of religion, concepts of love, sex and sin, inspiration and madness, the policing of thought, the conflict – yet again – of science and religion, and ideas of human nature, all invite attention.

The case of Christianity and its effect on the growth of knowledge is especially relevant. From the closing of the Schools of Athens through the Crusades and the Inquisition to the struggle with science in the modern period, Christianity has a central place in the history of knowledge in the West. The story of that relationship is germane to consideration of the future, for fundamentalist versions of Christianity and other religions are as active as ever in the great debate.

How has knowledge been passed on? Who decided in the past, and who decides now, what counts as knowledge? From Plato to the closing of the Academy, and from the new universities of medieval Christendom to the founding of public schools in England, the nature and purposes of education have been intensively debated. In all times education has been seen both as a threat to the established order and as the basis of utopian hopes.

But although quite a lot is known about the internal life of the educational process, and of how books, literacy, the transmission of knowledge and enquiry into new fields have played their part in the history of knowledge, and of how copyists, researchers, great teachers and heretics – many of whom died in the cause – made the history of knowledge possible, no one has yet (and we wait with impatience to see it) produced a single master-work telling that story as a whole.

It is a story that needs telling because two ideas – the idea of a curriculum (what pupils in an educational establishment should be taught, how and in what order) and of a canon (what truths – or, less tendentiously, texts – have to be known for a complete education) – are fundamental to the structure of a civilisation. It is one of the oddest quirks of history that this fact should now be so ill-understood, and that debate about education in the West has become a minor issue. In the past, control of the curriculum and canon – among other means, by the banning of books and the burning of teachers – was recognised as crucial. The reasons why, and the effect of recent emasculation of educational debate in the Anglophone world, repay study.

Yet other questions press. There have been many epochs in the history of knowledge, in the literal sense of periods of great change and importance. Dark nights of ignorance have fallen in regions of the world as a result of war or one or another kind of natural disaster, to be followed by renaissances and by struggle against the forces of ignorance which imposed, or were nurtured by, the preceding darker time. Some of the world's greatest civilisations withered and perished because they ceased to allow enquiry, challenge, argument and, therefore, growth; current civilisation seems to be under the same threat because, paradoxically, it knows too much of some things and – still – too little of others.

How did history, literature, art and new understandings of mankind – including those offered by medicine, magic and alchemy – happen? Each new departure in the development of these and other areas of knowledge represents a departure from a pre-existing state of what was taken for knowledge, and therefore the history of knowledge is in some sense a history of intellectual revolutions of the kind exemplified by classical Greek thought, the Renaissance, and the seventeenth-century scientific revolution.

The latter was a result of the success of method allied to a newly liberated spirit of enquiry. It has proved to be the dominating outlook of modern times. Here at least we have some answers to the central questions it prompts: how exactly are we to understand the scientific age we are living through, how does it work, in what way does the thinking characteristic of it differ from other kinds of thinking? What, in particular, can it tell us about the future of knowledge?

These questions are significant because they contrast with an arena of thought where mankind has been markedly less successful: the 'social sciences'. The histories of psychology and sociology and the development of economics from Adam Smith to Marshall, Keynes and beyond, prompt questions about government, social policy and 'social engineering'. How have these additions to knowledge – in some cases, *supposed* additions – affected the world? These themes converge, in an unexpected way, on such topics as advertising, propaganda and the idea of total war. And they form part of the redrawing of the map of intellectual history, because they consist of an effort to supply a want left by the abandonment of religious understandings of the world, namely, an explanation of, and a moral technology for, the non-material realities of human experience.

Every attempt at the growth of knowledge has been an attempt – so its champions saw it – to reach enlightenment. The concept of enlightenment was at times purloined by those who thought that magical or mystical shortcuts to it could be found. But in general the notion stands opposed to non-rational epistemic authorities such as faith, revelation and government by priesthoods.

The eighteenth century responded to the seventeenth century's scientific revolution by generalising science's sceptical and rational methods to debates about the moral realm, broadly conceived. Not everyone liked the results. Most histories of thought confine the Enlightenment with a capital 'E' to its eighteenth-century domicile in the Encyclopaedist movement, but this is a mistake: the grand ideological struggles of the nineteenth century, and the rise of 'post-modernist' styles of thought in the twentieth, are chapters in the same story.

That story is a continuation, in its own turn, of the War of Knowledge, with a new twist: one of the combatants now sees itself as human subjectivity struggling to preserve its sense of values against what it believes to be the blind and indifferent power of mechanised reason, levelling everything before it in the name of science. We are familiar with the world-view of Romanticism as it expressed itself in nineteenth-century poetry; but it comes as a surprise to realise – as we should – that post-modernist thought is romanticism in philosophy. From this insight hangs many a significant tale.

Much that this suggests about the history of knowledge might be construed as familiar, but the claim that to date it represents only the first tentative steps in mankind's progress is less so. At many points in history people have thought that they were present at an important, perhaps a perilous, juncture, and they were often right. Today, when both scientific knowledge and technological capacity are ready to expand in barely imaginable directions and with unstoppable rapidity – but with our social and political organisation, and our understanding of human psychology, still primitive and feeble – we seem to be at such another juncture, and perhaps an even more serious one. For the current combination is potentially disastrous, and sets mankind one of its greatest ever challenges.

Politically, human beings have advanced little from their long evolutionary history of conflict. They are still tribal, territorial and ready to kill one another for beliefs, and for control of goods and resources. Indeed, much of the world's wealth and energy is poured into arms and armies for these very reasons. But the growth of knowledge has replaced the spear with the computer-guided nuclear missile. This mixture of stone-age politics and contemporary science is, obviously, extraordinarily perilous. If humankind survives this phase – best done by finding the required political maturity – the world of the future will be as different from today as a computer is from a piece of flint. But if the history of knowledge provides any guide, it is likely that the required political maturity is still far to seek, and that there might be many steps backward before that future arrives – if ever it does.

The idea of a 'history of knowledge' involves an important assumption. Is there such a thing as knowledge – which is to say, truth? If not, can the idea of a 'growth of knowledge' make sense? To me it seems obvious that it does. But post-modernists argue against the idea of objective truth, and espouse relativism instead. On their view, there has been no growth of knowledge, only a succession of intellectual imperialisms: the ideology of the masters holds sway and passes for knowledge in its time. Is there any substance to this claim?

The history of ideas has also invited theories about the evolution of knowledge and science through history. There are, for example, progressivist theories like Hegel's, and 'axial' theories about 'crucial epochs' (just such a theory gives us our concepts of the Renaissance and the Enlightenment). A thorough enquiry into the growth of knowledge would explain and discuss these and other views, and test the idea that the history of knowledge is a single continuous tale of strife between, on the one hand, belief in the authority of reason and, on the other, beliefs to the effect that there are many other (and more important) sources of knowledge – for example revelation, faith, tradition, myths, mystical experience and the like.

As Goethe said, the story of the contest between reason and faith – which is what this strife ultimately comes down to – is one of the most important of all the stories we need to tell ourselves, and to understand aright, even while we live it.

And the point of all this is: that we need, more than ever, a history of knowledge, before ignorance has a chance to bring it to an end.

Perfect numbers:
a fragment of a tale

'Suppose I ask you,' Anselmo said, 'to think about the number six.' He stirred the fire with a stick of mimosa, a thin branch with a twist near the end. Now and then the tip caught a small lick of flame from the blaze, which Anselmo watched dispassionately for a moment before knocking it out.

Albertus thought about the number six.

'Twice three, thrice two, an even number, one less than a prime, the half of a dozen, the tenth part of sixty, which is the Babylonian Great Unit ——' he began.

'It is an interesting fact about numbers,' Anselmo interrupted, nodding appreciatively, 'that each one has so many fascinating properties. Do you notice that all the properties you mentioned are relational ones? I mean: what you tell me about six is how it relates to three and twelve and sixty and so forth. And that indeed, in the view of some, is the secret of numbers; though others will say there is something more to them.' He poked the fire again. 'Now, suppose I ask you to think about the numbers six and twenty-eight together.' He watched Albertus shrewdly from beneath his eyebrows, which made a luxuriant bushy screen for the purpose. As if reading aloud from a text inscribed in the fire, Albertus intoned:

'Both are even, their sum is thirty-four, their product is one hundred and sixty-eight, two is their lowest common denominator, the latter is two less than five times the former, and four greater than four times the former –' at which point Anselmo interrupted him again.

'Good! That is just how to start. But of course you are looking for a pattern.'

Albertus nodded.

'Do you see one?'

'Not yet,' Albertus said.

'There is one. Indeed there is a profound connection. No doubt you could get it just from thinking of the two of them alone, but it would help if I gave you a third number. In fact, it is the third in a series. It is four hundred and ninety-six.'

Albertus picked up his slate and wrote the three numbers down, one below the other.

'What I would like to know,' Anselmo continued, 'is what the sixth in this series is. The fourth was known to Euclid. I worked out the fifth for myself, a long time ago. Will you look for the sixth?'

Albertus nodded. After a moment he asked, 'Is it in the nature of the problem that it would be rather difficult to find the seventh, because of its size?'

Anselmo nodded in return.

Angelina broke the loaf into three and set the pieces down next to their bowls. They sat in silence for a moment, in the accustomed way, so that Angelina could say grace under her breath, and then Anselmo poured their wine. He said as he did so, 'Well, Albertus? You have that look about you: you have something to tell me.'

'I have,' Albertus replied. He marshalled his thoughts, and spoke on. 'The three numbers you gave me are all sums of their aliquots. In this they are very unusual, at least among the first thousand numbers; I find none others within that limit. Perhaps they grow more frequent; but from what you say about the difficulty of identifying them, perhaps not.'

'My boy!' said Anselmo warmly, 'my boy! Well done, well done indeed. You are exactly on track.' He clapped his hands. 'These numbers are the perfect numbers. They are the sums of their aliquots, as you say. Angelina? Can you see what is special about these numbers?'

'What numbers?' she asked, above the lip of her bowl.

'Six and twenty-eight. They are called perfect numbers. Can you think why?'

'Of course,' she said impatiently.

'Tell us.'

'God made the world in six days. He set the moon to go through its phases in twenty-eight days, which is therefore the rhythm of a woman too, as the lesser light. So the first number is the number of the beginning of things, and the second is the number of their continuation. It is quite proper that they should be called perfect.'

'Brava!' Anselmo said delightedly, clapping his hands again. 'Yours is the greater wisdom, Angelina, as ever and always.'

'But what is an aliquot?' she asked. 'It sounds like a fruit.'

'It is a part-without-remainder of a given number, other than that number itself. For example: the aliquot parts of 10 are 1, 2 and 5, because $1 = 10/10$, $2 = 10/5$, and $5 = 10/2$. Note that 10 is not an aliquot part of 10 since it is not a *proper quotient*, that is, a quotient different from the number itself.'

'And what has such a number to do with perfect numbers?' she asked.

'A perfect number,' Anselmo replied, 'is by definition a number which is equal to the sum of its aliquot parts. The first five are: 6; 28; 496; 8128; 33,550,336.'

Albertus had been sitting with furrowed brow during this exchange. He now said, 'And the sixth is: 8,589,869,056.'

It was Anselmo's turn to sit silent and still, his bowl halfway to his opened mouth, his eyes blank as he computed. He was not as quick as Albertus at this task, but the contents of his bowl were still warm when he cried, 'Yes!'

But of course Albertus was ahead of him still. 'And the seventh,' he said, licking the rim of his bowl, 'is 137,438,691,328.'

'So you have a method!' Anselmo said eagerly.

'Take any sequence of numbers,' Albertus replied, nodding, 'starting from 1 and doubling its predecessor, such that their sum is a prime; multiply the prime by the last term in the sequence; and the result is a Perfect Number.'

Anselmo quickly tried the method on the known numbers, and nodded in his turn, his eyes gleaming in the firelight.

Angelina, who had been listening with interest, said, 'Yes, I see: 1+2+4=7; 7×4=28; 28 is a perfect number. Easy.'

'Easy,' Anselmo and Albertus agreed, saying the word simultaneously, and laughing with pleasure. Their laughter drifted into the night, beyond the flickering light of their fire as it touched leaves and tree-trunks in the thick darkness of the surrounding wood, where the eyes of enemy spies watched them, and evil spirits hovered in wait.

POLEMICS

Answering critics

Good reviews of course please writers greatly, but not as greatly as bad reviews upset them. Writers are an irritable tribe, and remember the latter with tenacity and bitterness long after good reviews are forgotten. Since it is a rare book that does not encounter at least one reviewer with a hangover, or who has just had a domestic quarrel, or who has been selected by a review editor for known antipathy to the author, it is a rare scribbler who does not carry somewhere the quietly or otherwise suppurating wound inflicted by barbs of criticism.

Since all authors have their share of such, they do best to accept them as hazards of the trade. The chief reason is the obvious one that no one can please everyone all the time, and in any case there are people out there who refuse to be pleased. So the barbs will come among the bouquets, and must be borne in the flesh, sometimes forever.

Two classes of my own critics cause me amusement rather than otherwise, for which I owe them gratitude. One consists in folk of a religious turn of mind, who are annoyed by my dislike of religion and my attacks upon it, on the grounds of its falsehood, its moralising oppressiveness and the terrible conflicts it has caused throughout history, and causes still. These critics call me dogmatic, narrow-minded, intolerant and unfair in what I say about their superstitions and the systems of moral tyranny erected upon them. Well: as experts in dogma and narrow-mindedness, they are doubtless in a good position to recognise it when they find it.

But I answer as follows. I believe in pluralism and the tolerance that alone makes pluralism workable, yes. But valuing tolerance does not mean accepting that anything goes. For example, believing in tolerance does not oblige one to tolerate murder, or folly or superstitious and fanciful world-views directly descended from the ignorance of the cave-man (which is what religion is). What the evidence of history and reason shows to be an evil in the world, one must oppose: and where the evil is great, it must be opposed robustly. So those who believe in, and base their lives upon, the ancient fairy tales that once constituted all that human beings possessed in the way of science, technology, psychology, history and philosophy, and which has since been vastly superseded, cannot expect their absurdities to be handled with kid-gloves, not least because almost all of them try to foist their outlook on others; and far too many of them, throughout history and still today, are prepared to coerce or even kill those who do not agree.

Unlike the espousers of these absurdities, many of whom are avowedly intolerant of different beliefs or none, I am prepared to tolerate their existence, if they practise their religion in quietness and do not impose themselves upon others. Religion is like sex: it is mostly for the privacy of the closet (though public sex as entertainment is acceptable – far more so than religion), and when it takes aberrant forms or leaks into the open in disruptive ways it should be abated. But on the excellent grounds noted above, I hold that what religious people think and do is ridiculous and too often dangerous, which makes combating it a duty.

The other class of critic consists of those few among my fellow academic philosophers who think that speaking or writing in ways that the wider public can understand is a matter for resentment. One such lately asked what the point was of my writing short essays about moral and social topics, of the kind and length that suit a newspaper column. This suggests that, like others of the group in question, this critic thinks that the only 'real' philosophy is to be done in the elaborate technical jargon of journal papers or scholarly monographs, the vast majority of which are read by very few, and exceedingly rarely by non-academics. The implication of this is that unless the newspapers will take 5,000-word-long articles bulging with immense words, minute distinctions and a supporting apparatus of footnotes and references, there should be no mention of philosophical ideas in the public arena.

Actually, this critic did allow that if you were a very well-known and now dead philosopher called Bertrand Russell (who at one time wrote a 600-word weekly column for the Hearst newspapers in America, on topics like wearing lipstick and teaching children how to be hypocritical – some of them rather good), and if you deliberately wrote in highly paradoxical and provocative vein as Russell did, then you could be allowed to get away with it. Alas, we cannot all be great dead philosophers while we live, so we must bear with being deprecated for following the example of what Russell and many other great dead philosophers did: namely, write for their fellows in society, and not just the self-elected few who affect to know the difference between the cosmological argument and the cosmological constant.

There is, though, something not just ungenerous but unworthy about people so nervous about the value of what they do, yet so jealous of their prerogatives in doing it, that at all costs they must not stoop to share it with outsiders – and nor must their colleagues. The disparagement directed by such at the enterprise of philosophising in accessible ways, as the first invitation to everyone to explore the rich resource of philosophical thought, betrays an unhealthy preciosity. Looked at down their long and disapproving noses, the art involved, and the good that might be done, in following Russell's example must always be a blur, if visible at all. One's sympathy for these myopics is tempered, though, by the fact that they do not wish others to see clearly either: and there lies the pity of it.

Biotechnology and policy

If you were asked how public policy debate about bio-technology differs in three of the world's leading economies – say, the United States, the United Kingdom and Germany – a moment's reflection would bring a set of obvious points to mind.

In the United States organised and vociferous religious lobbies have a large impact on debate about abortion, assisted fer-tilisation, embryo research and cloning. By contrast, genetic modification of foodstuffs worries relatively few people. Com-mercial imperatives count for most, though, and in the key matter of patenting biotechnological entities and techniques in anticipation of commercial exploitation of them, the United States leads the world.

In the United Kingdom, with its pragmatically conservative public policy environment, a cautious and piecemeal accept-ance – within negotiated limits – of abortion, assisted fer-tilisation, embryo research and cloning is in place, but a well-organised and vociferous Green lobby has opposed the commercial exploitation of genetically modified (GM) crops. Because of anxieties prompted by analogies this lobby can draw with the 'mad cow disease' crisis, its opposition to GM tech-nology has touched a loud chord among many.

In Germany the cold memory of Nazism makes biotechnology as applied to human beings a much more vexed topic. This does not apply to GM crops and foods, to which German attitudes are shaped by acceptance, without the felt need for much debate, of general EU regulations about novel foodstuffs and labelling.

But anything that calls to mind eugenics and other real or imagined implications of biotechnological advances can touch sensitive nerves, and one of the results is that German debate about such matters is self-censored and has the air of 'not mentioning the elephant in the room'.

Such are the things one might immediately say when invited to reflect on the differences in the reception and handling of biotechnological advances in these three large economies wrought by differences in their national and political culture.

The interest in comparing attitudes to biotechnology around the world arises from the light to be cast on one or more of the following: the differences in history and political culture which explain the variations in the way countries manage bio-technology's threats and promises; the arguments, both ethical and pragmatic, adduced in each for and against the acceptance of biotechnological techniques and practices; what is actually happening in the scientific work being done in different countries in the light of these other differences; the commercial imperatives involved, and the pressure exerted by the likelihood that states with far laxer political and ethical concerns about biotechnology (for example, China) will forge ahead; and, not least, the medical, social and economic promise held out in so many ways by biotechnology.

No one has yet done a thorough analysis of these differences, but one thing at least is clear: biotechnology is as big a Next Big Thing as information and communication technology, and is sure to have an even more profound effect on the future of humanity. Countries that lag behind in the biotech science and policy arenas will suffer for it in the new world dawning; and it is those that have most to lose in the way of tradition and superstition who will lag furthest behind.

Moral outrage

Outrage has a long history. It is the starting point for two of civilisation's earliest literary classics: the *Iliad* and the Bible. In the first, Achilles is outraged because Agamemnon confiscates one of his slave-girls. In *Genesis*, a later work than the *Iliad*, Adam and Eve outrage God by eating forbidden fruit, and in revenge he curses all mankind forever.

With such precedents it is no surprise that the British have always been good at outrage. King John's barons were outraged by his taxes, so in 1215 they forced Magna Carta upon him. Parliament was outraged by Charles I's attempt to override it, so in 1649 it removed his head. In 1739 the whole nation was so outraged that a Spaniard had cut off a British sailor's ear that it went to war.

But it took the Victorian era to refine outrage into specifically moral outrage, with sex and nudity as the chief targets, and offences against religion close behind. In 1877 Annie Besant outraged public sensibility by publishing a birth-control pamphlet, and nearly went to prison. In 1881 Ibsen's *Ghosts* was staged in London to cries of horror over its supposedly sordid themes. In 1885 a fierce correspondence broke out in *The Times* following a letter from 'A British Matron', who complained of an exhibition of nude paintings which 'revolted the sense of public decency' (i.e. *her* anxieties and timidities about naked flesh).

In this climate it was unsurprising that Thomas Hardy's *Jude the Obscure* should be greeted with outrage on its publication in 1895; even his wife Emma objected, and the Bishop of Wakefield threw it into his fireplace. Hardy never wrote another novel.

Victorian sensibility did not end with Victoria's death. In the 1920s a crusadingly moralistic Home Secretary, William Joynson-Hicks, banned Joyce's *Ulysses* and Radclyffe Hall's *The Well of Loneliness*. D. H. Lawrence's *Lady Chatterley's Lover* provoked huge moral outrage, and even when its publication became possible in 1960 the climate had not changed enough to prevent more outrage at Kenneth Tynan's *Oh Calcutta!* in 1967, nor the posture of moral outrage manfully sustained by Mary Whitehouse for most of the decades that followed.

What moral outrage always aims at is censorship. Recently the play *Behzti* was silenced by the moral outrage of Sikhs in Birmingham. Predictably, the objecting Sikhs had not seen the play, yet knew that it absolutely had to close. The same impulse attended the outrage over the BBC's airing of *Jerry Springer: The Opera*.

A mature society is one that reserves its moral outrage for what really matters: poverty and preventable disease in the third world, arms sales, oppression, injustice. Bad language and sex might offend some, who certainly have a right to complain; but they do not have a right to censor. They do not have to watch or listen if they are offended: they have an 'off' button on their television sets and radios. After all, it is morally outrageous that moral outrage should be used as an excuse to perpetrate the outrage of censorship on others.

Science and modern times

Modern times and the rise of science are the same thing. For convenience the year 1600 could be nominated as their joint birthday, although the preceding gestation had been long, and it was not until late in the century that the first true classic of science – Newton's *Principia* – appeared.

But in the early decades of the century there were two outstanding figures who between them shed light that helped others see the scientific path ahead. They were Francis Bacon and René Descartes. Neither made lasting scientific discoveries as such (though Descartes left a legacy to mathematics), but each examined the crucial matter of how inquiry should proceed.

In their day thinkers did not differentiate between chemistry and alchemy, astrology and astronomy, medicine and magic. Bacon and Descartes in their respective ways showed how to winnow the grain of knowledge from the chaff of nonsense. To them, therefore, is owed the first steps in true scientific method, which now, in its ideal application, involves the scrupulous testing of hypotheses by evidence, openness to public assessment of results, and readiness to revise or abandon theories in the light of new or better data.

As one would expect from the co-operative use of disciplined, sober and educated intelligence, the resulting achievements have been breathtaking, and have transformed the world for the good in all respects other than those in which politics and business have misapplied them.

Against the background of these thoughts it is instructive to consider three news stories, printed as it happens on the same page in the same newspaper, which appeared on the day that these words were written. One was a report from a scientific conference in Seattle, where the discovery was announced of a remote galaxy. It lies at a distance of 13 billion light years, which puts it almost at the edge of the universe. Because distance is time in cosmological terms, to look at it is thus to see right back to a period only 750 million years after the Big Bang. The galaxy was detected by the Hubble space telescope, and Hubble's observations were confirmed by the Keck observatory on Hawaii.

The second news story reported the result of a poll conducted for ABC News in the United States, which showed that a majority of Americans believe that the earth was created in six days, that Moses parted the Red Sea, and that Noah and his family survived the Flood in the ark, accompanied by the world's animals in pairs.

E. M. Forster's motto was 'only connect'. After pondering the juxtaposition of these two stories for a while, one about fundamental science and the other about fundamentalist belief, one might turn, in the interests of making connections, to the third news story. This reported that despite the successes of the Western powers in Afghanistan, women there were still in thrall to the oppressions of a religious morality which condemned them to captivity, exploitation, indignity and death.

Girls were still married to adult men at ages as young as eight. A sixteen-year-old girl who fled her eighty-five-year-old husband was arrested and sent to prison for doing so. In Herat any woman found with a male companion not related to her by blood or marriage was subjected to a virginity examination. In many places in Afghanistan women were still barred from education. Every twenty minutes of every day an Afghan woman died in childbirth, and half of all women died in the course of one of their multiple (the average is eight) pregnancies.

These dismal data from a part of the world where religion was then (and alas is, largely, still) the only science remind one of an uncomfortable fact. Everywhere that religion has ever held temporal power, the result has approximated Taliban-style rule. We forget, in the West, how much it took to escape orthodoxy enforced by burnings at the stake, and how recently: indeed, at the beginnings of modern times with the rise of science.

It is said that we shall know a thing by its fruits. A striking fact about the adventure of science, whenever it escapes the attentions of those who pervert it to making war rather than progress, is how well it serves mankind. Think of X-ray machines, social science research into human welfare, the appliances of leisure that fill our homes with colourful entertainments and music: it is hard not to make comparisons between a world ameliorated by these things and any world shaped by taking as true the bleak and desperate ignorances of ancient legends.

Critics of these thoughts will say that they are severely tendentious: 'science is good except when bad,' says the above, and critics will point to Hiroshima and Zyklon B in Auschwitz as proof that this is an effort to get science off too lightly. At the same time they defend religion by pointing to the ceiling of the Sistine Chapel, the sacred cantatas of Bach, the comfort it gives to the old and lonely, and the acts of benevolence it can inspire.

But the express implication of the points made earlier is that despite these positives, there are otherwise precious few ways in which religion does not do serious disservice to mankind, and many ways in which the benefits of science outweigh the disservice it can be misapplied to do. The defenders of religion point to the Sistine Chapel and Bach's cantatas, and the solace afforded the old and lonely, as a kind of equivalence to the payoff of science's positive fruits against nuclear weapons and Zyklon B. For even if religious art (invariably a product of devotion? or of the fact that the Church had the money to commission it?)

and the deceiving solaces are counted into the equation, the massive burden of conflict, psychological no less than in the way of wars, inquisitions, crusades, burnings of heretics and the rest – egregious among them the Holocaust – for which religion is directly and indirectly responsible, makes for a massive weight of harm to humanity which dwarfs these benefits. Accordingly it would be a bold individual who sought to claim that, just as the hundreds of millions saved by (say) antibiotics can be invoked as some compensation for the (say) millions whom advanced weaponry has killed (adamantly granting that *one* person thus killed is too many), so the Sistine Chapel and someone's comfort at having a bible under his pillow make the historical excesses of (say) anti-Semitism acceptable, to say nothing of the wholesale enslavement of mankind to falsity, which religion by its nature seeks to impose, and too often succeeds. (And here one sees how hollowly it would ring to say 'and just *one* person thus victimised would be too many' – for religion does the contrary of concede that this is victimisation.)

One key consideration is the massive and systematic falsity of views to the effect that supernatural agencies operate in the universe with express reference to the lives of human beings on this planet, given in addition that they are so often and widely invoked to direct, dominate and often distort those lives. Consider the contrast between this and science.

Science labours towards an understanding of things, testing itself vigorously and on the way (directly and indirectly – to re-employ this phrase – this latter via technologies) affecting the lives of billions every day. One can confidently reassert that the good versus harm balance lies hugely in its favour in this, as witness the commonplace example of its effects – say, electricity: the electricity that pumps water to your house, lights and heats it, cooks your food, puts you in touch with your family and friends, brings you news and entertainment – all and every day. When last did it guide a missile your way, or communicate itself to you via a torturer's cattle prod? These things tragically happen, and they are indeed applications – misapplications – of science; but though a defender of religion can rightly say that to play a numbers game is crude, it is relevant. For the dozens of mutually blaspheming and non-rationally-based religions, each claiming final and uncontestable truth on the basis of supposed revelations communicated two or more thousand years ago, live off their falsehood continuously, invoke it and rely upon it daily, and use it to motivate antipathies and conflicts as well as to encourage benignities; though even as regards this latter one would surely wish to see people encouraged to kindness and concern by feelings of humanity rather than by fairy stories (or rewards in heaven, whether or not in the form of the attentions of seventy-two virgins).

This acknowledges the point that religion – these false views of the universe – can give comfort and inspiration, and prompt many acts of benevolence. One would surely wish comfort and inspiration to everyone, and applaud any act of benevolence: but still prefer that their motivation not be falsely based. And of course, uncountable acts of benevolence are performed by non-believers too, perhaps more admirably still, since humanity alone (if it is truly benevolence in the case) is the impulse.

It is in the light of this contrast between science and religion that the remarks in the first half of this piece were written. Hence the complete confidence that if one throws the net wide (for example, to include the Holocaust as one of the legacies of religion), what it catches in the respective cases is sharply different in overall character. The argument that officially atheistic communism 'has killed more people than all holy wars and holy tortures' (to quote a debating partner) repeats a canard. Was it communism's atheism that prompted the massacre of Kulaks or the starvation of Chinese peasants in the Great Leap

Forward, or might it have been the ideology of class war and theories about collectivisation? Where did communism learn its lessons about prophets and holy books, orthodoxy and conformity, and the need to put heretics to death? On what did it model its eschatological picture of human history, its call for suffering now in the interests of a utopian future, its preparedness to kill and die for the faith?

Those less reflective about the nuances of history blame communism (and fascism) on the Enlightenment, failing to see that the secular, democratic and humanist offspring of Enlightenment refused to accept either fascism or communism, and defeated the former in seventeen years and the latter in seventy. For both are in fact counter-Enlightenment movements, sharing more in common with the forms of religion from which they borrowed their lineaments – the oppression of a monolithic world-view premised on a fairy tale about origins, destiny and the right morality required for salvation – than with the pluralist, open, educated, liberal society based on rights and opportunities envisioned by the eighteenth century's *philosophes*. Yes, this is yet to come, if ever it will; but look at the forces opposing it even as these words are written: Southern Baptists, radical Islamists.

New Age religion

In the United States and Nigeria religious observance is increasing. In mature, world-wise, sophisticated Western Europe, attendance at church has long been declining. But declining European church attendance does not mean a reduction in superstitious belief. It has partially been offset by interest in New Age alternatives. Thus some non-churchgoers buy crystals, have their astrological charts cast, and arrange their houses according to feng-shui principles. (To add a characteristic further touch of contradiction, they might yet remain 'C of E' – 'Christmas and Easter' – nevertheless.)

One thing this change in ways of expressing credulity does is to show that religion is in essence no different from these other observances. The shift really comes down to rejecting participation in *organised* religion in favour of vaguer, less demanding and more exotic superstitions. A recent BBC survey on religion in Britain showed that almost half of the population claim to believe in the existence of some kind of 'higher power'. This degree of residual superstition explains why Mel Gibson's film *The Passion of the Christ* struck a chord with some when it first appeared. (According to his own testimony, Mr Gibson is a practising Roman Catholic and his wife is a practising Anglican. Asked whether he agreed with his denomination's doctrine that 'there is no salvation outside the Church' he said he did; which meant – he further explained – that he had to accept that although his wife was a better person than himself, he was saved and she was not. Such, one sees, is true religion.)

Although Western Europeans inhabit a post-Christian culture, the symbols and stories of the Christian tradition still exert emotional power among them. The reason has less to do with that tradition itself than the tradition to which it itself belongs. Stories of the death and resurrection of gods are very ancient. They can be traced back through all middle-eastern mythologies to ancient Egypt. Gods such as Horus, heroes such as Odysseus, and symbolic figures such as Orpheus, all went to the underworld for various reasons, and returned. The earliest myths were prompted by the death of vegetation in winter and its resurrection in spring. The Jesus legend is a version of that mythic tradition. People today only know the Christian version, and identify with it because it is central to the institution which for 1500 years dominated much of European and therefore Western history: the Church.

The 'Passion' story – the trial and death of Jesus – has a grip on people's minds largely because of the horror of the story. In medieval times practically every church had murals depicting it in full colour. The Alte Pinakothek in Munich has an overwhelming collection of altarpieces from that period in which one can see, portrayed with ghoulish relish, cruel scenes of suffering and agony, with gushing blood, livid wounds, faces awash with tears, much weeping and wailing. Alongside were pictures showing the torments of hell awaiting those who would not respond suitably to all the suffering alleged to have taken place on their behalf. The coercive and ugly aesthetic of most Christian history and teaching – replaced (now that the doctrine has to compete with alternatives and indifference) by saccharine images of Mary and a baby, and statuettes of the Bleeding Heart in which Jesus's eyes are turned mournfully upwards like a spaniel's – is not now fully appreciated. But the icon of a tortured semi-naked corpse hanging on a scaffold remains the central image, intended to provoke – well, whatever response is supposed to be central to that queer religion.

People seem to have a psychological need for images that convey gripping, scary, upsetting ideas. It does not really matter what images succeed in stimulating us to feel these emotions, as the great variety of horror films shows. Our cultural heritage has conditioned us to think that the crucifixion is especially emblematic, because the corpse's suffering is said to have been a sacrifice for others. Mothers suffer sacrificially a great deal of the time, of course, and repeated experiences of giving birth (say – a twelve-hour or more labour) would not be hard to calibrate against a one-off experience of three hours nailed to planks of wood. Nor would the last months of terminal cancer, thoughtfully provided, so some allege, by the Intelligent Designer of the universe. But the idea of the Passion is nevertheless taken to be especially iconic, holding its votaries by engendering a blend of curiosity and superstitious awe.

The Passion story comes from a literature that was written at particular times for particular people. The first canonical gospel, the one according to Mark, was written in Rome about AD 60 soon after Jerusalem was sacked. It was pitched at a Roman audience who asked the question, 'Why should we take seriously the story of someone who was executed by our authorities as a political rebel?' (Crucifixion was the specific method of execution for terrorists and insurgents.) The answer Mark gave was that the Jewish Sanhedrin tricked the Romans into crucifying Jesus. From then until very recently (and, for some, still) the Jews were the murderers of the Messiah, and were accordingly demonised – and viciously persecuted – by Christianity.

When a religious organisation has political as well as spiritual authority it increasingly tends to adopt a repressive and tyrannical Taliban-like face. The orthodox (which means: those with power) persecute the heterodox and unbelievers, even to the extent of torturing and killing them. One has only to think of the Inquisition and the Wars of Religion that followed the

Reformation: if a person disagreed with the Church he could be burned at the stake – and many were. Now the situation is different. The Churches are in retreat, so they have turned themselves into organisations full of brotherly love and charity. In this friendly mode they seek to play down the horrors of their past, and gloss over their murderous relationship with Judaism. The Church has gone from harshness to happy hymns, from Savonarola to snappy sermons, from punishment to the persuasion of marketing ploys.

Would the Christian Churches stay the same – 'happy clappy hymns' – if ever they regained the degree of power of life and death, of torture on the rack and burning at the stake, that they once wielded over our daily lives? One very profoundly doubts it.

Divorce

Is monogamy a good thing? It is not – at least, when properly understood.

In the business of analysing important ideas, the dividing line between precision and logic-chopping is so fine that it is often invisible. No doubt many readers of the argument I put forward in the paragraphs to follow will think that I have not just crossed the line but travelled far beyond into the realms of casuistry.

They will think this because, as invariably happens, the name of an important idea – here 'monogamy' – comes to serve as shorthand for a variety of associated ideas, and the attitudes they prompt, which they take themselves to be talking about when they use the word; and when they are reminded that the strict and literal content of the concept in question is not what they habitually mean, they think they are being practised upon.

But all concepts that play central roles in shaping our social mores and personal relationships need to be examined with scrupulous exactness, so that the tangled penumbra of associated ideas – associated for historical and adventitious reasons far more often than for logical ones – can cease to obscure the central issue.

Thus it matters that I should state straight away that in arguing *against* monogamy I am not therefore arguing *for* polygamy, nor *for* sexual infidelity or promiscuity. People can argue in favour of polygamy or promiscuity, and might make excellent cases for either or both; but that is not what I am doing here.

Here, rather, I argue that monogamy, properly and strictly understood, is a bad thing; and for the following reasons.

The word 'monogamy' derives from the two Greek words *monos* meaning 'one', 'only' or 'sole', and *gamos* meaning 'marriage'. Etymologically, therefore, 'monogamy' means 'one marriage'. By itself the phrase is ambiguous between 'one marriage at a time' meaning 'one (official) spouse at a time', and 'one marriage (one spouse) in a lifetime'. To determine which is the primary meaning, one has to look at the history of the word's application. And it quickly becomes clear that it is the second of these meanings that is primary.

This is shown by the Christian doctrine of marriage (leaving aside the convenient amendments of annulment and permission to marry after the death of a spouse), which says that once the deity has made a man and woman one flesh, they are never to be sundered. This remains Roman Catholic doctrine, and is implicit in the hand-wringing in the Church of England over second marriages in church. It is implicit too in the practices of other traditions; for one example, *suttee* in Hinduism is an unequivocal expression of the idea that *monos gamos* means what it says: one marriage per lifetime.

There are of course traditions which affirm monogamy, in the sense of allowing individuals to marry only once, but which permit a man to have, in addition to his official wife, concubines or sexually available slaves, or (in Europe, and less officially) a mistress or mistresses. This was the case in antiquity, both Judaic and Greek, and in China until very recently. Contrast this arrangement with that in Islam, in which a man is permitted to have up to four wives specifically to avoid infidelity and promiscuity, the thought being that a sufficient plurality of wives will leave neither need nor energy for either. This shows that the concepts of 'infidelity', 'sexual variety', 'promiscuity', 'monogamy' need to be kept strictly distinct, because they do not mutually imply one another's affirmation or negation, even if for historico-sociological reasons they frequently suggest one another.

But although there are monogamous traditions in which the legal state of marriage is separated from the number and character of sexual arrangements that accompany it, in the Western tradition the strict sense of monogamy is intended to convey oneness of spouse or sexual partner as well as oneness of engagement in the legal state of marriage. It is this sense of 'monogamy' that I shall now show is a bad thing.

People grow and change. Through experience they acquire new needs, interests and perceptions. They outlive marriages, especially those contracted when relatively young. To condemn people to remain in a relationship which seemed good at one time but which by a later time has become a painful straitjacket, a mutually toxic and life-denying source of chronic unhappiness, seems as cruel as it is stupid. For individual well-being and flourishing, it is essential that people should be able to forge new intimacies when old ones have died. This is true even when there are children in the case, since a persistently unhappy home environment can damage children, while happier second relationships can show them that marriage with the right person in the right way can constitute one of life's central amenities.

Does one need to say more than that? To be *against monogamy* (properly understood) is no more nor less than to be *for divorce and the permissibility and acceptability of remarriage.* And the case for this has surely long since been accepted by all rational folk. For, baldly considered, the spurious metaphysics of religious arguments against divorce and remarriage are an antiquated irrelevance. The prudential arguments about staying married for the sake of children, though far weightier, are only prudential; if staying together does children more harm than good, the marriage should end; and anyway the most that such an argument could enjoin is that parents remain together until children leave home.

So, monogamy – the circumstance of being permitted only one spouse per lifetime, *pace* death or the Jesuitries of annulment and the like – is a bad thing. But this, to repeat, does not automatically imply any positive thesis about relationship behaviour, such as polygamy or promiscuity, for each of the varieties of which a separate case has to be made. It only implies that Milton was long ago right: divorce should be available for the happiness of humankind.

Self-education

When new school years begin each balmy month of September, they unwittingly reinforce a common but usually unvoiced assumption: that education belongs to the young, who must get it in formally constituted places of study. But is it only the young who should be going back to school come each succeeding summer's end? Surely everyone should, though of course not only or even necessarily in institutions. For education is an attitude: the streets are a classroom to the observant eye, and in every bookshop and library banquets of knowledge lie waiting.

If there is a single subject which embraces everything else in it, and which at the same time is a delight to study – for studying it involves nothing other than immersing oneself in stories about events and people; and, typically, great events and remarkable people – it is history. Not only does history incorporate science, politics, war, psychology, sociology, geography and law, but as the sum and head of them all it constitutes philosophy too. 'History,' said Thucydides, 'is philosophy teaching by example.'

As all roads lead to Rome, so following any thread leads to history. Take so simple a thing as the date of the day these words were written – 9 September. That is Chrysanthemum Day in Japan, one of five seasonal feasts, associated with the Japanese royal family because the chrysanthemum is its emblem, representative of the sun. According to the *Kojiki*, the chronicles of ancient Japan, the sun goddess Amaterasu

Omikami fashioned the imperial insignia and gave them to her grandson Ninigi no Mikoto, who in turn bequeathed them to his descendants, the emperors, along with magical and priestly powers. These divine attributes put the emperors above sublunary matters, so the government of the kingdom was left to ministers, for most of the country's history the Shoguns of ferocious memory.

Another 9 September was the day in 1513 when an English army led by the Earl of Surrey beat the Scots under King James IV at Flodden Field, occasioning the beautiful lament 'The Flowers of the Forest', bewailing the best young men of Scotland who lay 'cauld in the clay' as a result. James had invaded England because his brother-in-law Henry VIII had invaded France, and James felt the claims of the old alliance between Scotland and France to be stronger than the family bond. Flodden was a turning-point in military history: it was the last battle in which the longbow played a part, and the first in which artillery was significant. Unhappily for the Scots, they had been equipped by the French with the long pike, a formidable weapon against cavalry but useless in close-quarter fighting. Surrey's men slaughtered Scotland's nobility and the prime of its youth that day. Scotland's eventual conquest of England had to wait the more peaceful outcome of the union between James VI and Henry VIII's sister Margaret, in the form of James 'I and VI' in 1603.

The Battle of Flodden took place on a Friday. In 1547 9 September was also a Friday, as we know from the diary of William Patten, a kind of latter-day Aulus Gellius – a miscellaneous writer, a collector of unconsidered trifles, and a puzzler over the meaning of things. In his entry for this date Patten noted that it was the feast-day of a neglected saint, St Gorgon. He wrote, 'This day is marked in the calendar with the name of saint Gorgon, no famous saint sure, either so obscure that no man knows him, or else so ancient as every man forgets him.' He went on to wonder whether St Gorgon was odiferous, as suggested by a line in one of Horace's 'Sermones': 'Rufillus smells of breath-fresheners, Gorgonius smells of billy-goat.' Patten's ingenuous belief that a Latin poet might be writing about a Christian saint is rather charming; perhaps he mistook the meaning of the word 'sermones', which is not 'sermons' but 'satires'.

And so one could multiply examples from almost any starting point. Apart from the entertainment value, the moral is that every glimpse into the past proves rich in instruction. Remembering the events of a single day, as with the anniversary of Flodden Field, opens the door to a complete tranche of time; and the connections from that time to the present are many and educative.

Writing during the Second World War, E. M. Forster observed that people who were afraid of their sergeant-majors could turn to the history books and lord it over kings and generals, judging this one a fool and that one a knave depending upon the suggestions offered by that most luxurious of commodities, hindsight. Hindsight might not invariably help with foresight, though it is our only resource in that department; but it certainly enriches understanding of the present, which is the very least that continuing education is for.

Face transplants

When the first-ever (partial) face transplant took place, performed by a team of French surgeons on a woman whose face had been mauled by a dog, immediate reactions predictably focused on matters of ethics. Scarcely mentioned is the hope that the procedure gave to tens of thousands of severely disfigured people, victims of burn and blast injuries and shootings, who rarely leave their homes to avoid the misery of being stared at as freaks.

Critics of face transplantation describe it as a 'quality-of-life' procedure as contrasted to a life-saving one. This implies that it is a relatively unimportant medical measure, not too far in status from 'mere' cosmetic surgery. What this fails to recognise is that life is very much a matter of its quality, so the default reaction to anything that improves quality of life, especially for those denied the chance of ordinary activities and relationships by the way they look, should be to see it as indeed a life-saver – a saver of normal life – and to welcome it accordingly. This point applies to plastic and cosmetic surgery generally, but surely most of all to face transplantation.

It emerged in press coverage of the first face transplant that the thirty-eight-year-old Frenchwoman whose nose, lips and chin had been bitten off by her dog was unconscious when it happened, because she had attempted suicide and the dog was trying to rouse her. This news deepened concerns about whether the woman would be able to negotiate the potentially grave psychological difficulties anticipated even for mentally robust recipients of transplants.

This consideration was subjoined to other ethical concerns. One was whether the woman had been in a position to give properly informed consent, in light of her traumatised state and the fact that her surgeons could give no assurances about the outcome. Another is whether she should first have been offered reconstructive plastic surgery. Transplant surgery carries far higher risks because the patient's immune system has to be suppressed to lessen the danger of donor tissue rejection. If the microsurgical connections of blood capillaries and nerves did not work, the donated tissue might die, leaving the patient in a worse state than before. Reconstruction is more conservative, though in theory transplants promise much better aesthetic results.

The medical success or failure of individual face transplants is one thing; the general psychological and philosophical questions prompted by them are another. It is these that have excited most debate since doctors first announced that face transplants are surgically feasible.

One point that can be left aside immediately is the science-fiction possibility that a whole face transplant would result in the familiar face of a dead relative appearing unchanged on the front of a stranger's head. This grotesque-seeming scenario was the cause of much initial revulsion towards the idea of face transplantation. But on the best supposition, successfully transferring muscle, fat, cartilage and skin constituting one person's face onto the skull of another person would result in a greatly changed appearance because of the different shape and size of the underlying bone structure.

Moreover the play of expression on the face would owe everything to the mind animating it. As actors – and portrait painters and photographers – know, a person's habitual look can be remarkably different from their appearance in repose. Some people are unrecognisable in the fixedness of a photograph for this reason. For an allied reason, a person's look is much more a matter of habitual expression – the way the face is composed by the emotions and the mindset governing it – than mere superficial structure.

There is accordingly little risk of a face staying the same when it is moved to someone else's head. The real problem lies with the insides of the heads of wearers of new faces, for they have to deal with the considerable psychological challenges thus posed. Those challenges relate chiefly to the sense of self, of identity, and of answers to the question 'who am I and who do others think I am?' that help to constitute that sense.

The task of refashioning a sense of identity is not as unfamiliar a one in human experience as one might think. It is in its way a rather common one, because it is not restricted to people whose looks have been changed by injury or disease. Ageing provides a powerful example. Many people become acutely conscious, at a certain point in middle life, that the visage in the bathroom mirror no longer conforms to the mental picture they have of themselves. They can sometimes be horrified to find that the stranger approaching them in a shopfront window is their own reflection.

Even in these cases the difficulty of adjustment should not be underestimated. It is a central component of the midlife crises blamed for many a husband's marriage-destroying flight with his secretary. But in the case of injury or disease the adjustment required is greater; and greater again is likely to be the adjustment required following a face transplant.

For one thing, some recipients of donor organs find it hard to live with the thought that someone else's body parts are grafted to them. Some recipients of limbs have later requested their amputation because of a sense of the donated limb's foreignness. To a certain sort of imagination, having the whole or part of someone else's face attached in place of one's own original one just seems horrifying.

Secondly, the recipient of a transplant is not the only one who has to get used to it. In making their own adjustments, family and friends have to guard against anything in their own reactions that undermine the recipient's mental progress in accepting the change. That is likely to be hard work for the family, because for them it is not like having a new person in the house – a relatively easy innovation to accept – but a familiar person in a disconcerting, ambiguous guise.

Still, it has to be remembered that the transplanted face would (if successful) be giving a normal look to what, before the operation, was an appearance disfigured enough to warrant a transplant; and the difficulty of living with disfigurement, for both the subject and his family, is likely to be greater than getting used to a new but conventionally acceptable appearance. Moreover, the recipient would be buoyed by the positive aspects of the change, even though confronted with the difficult business of getting used to it.

That difficulty will concern not just the points about identity already made, but the new situation which the change of appearance brings into being. The complex factors that give a person his sense of self include the way others treat him, react to him, read his expressions, and respond to how he presents himself in public – for this, even in the first few seconds of a first encounter, provides others with much of the grounds on which they make their judgements about him. The self-image in part built out of the way others approach him will undergo a transformation only hinted at by what recipients of radical makeovers in TV shows experience, or by people who disguise themselves as old folk or members of the opposite sex to see what it is like to walk in someone else's shoes. Reports by people who have tried these latter temporary experiments make striking reading; only consider what it must be like to know that the changes in question are permanent. To get a sense of these, one might have to consult the experience of transsexuals.

But if one thing is certain about the identity problem, it is that there is little question that recipients of a face transplant would feel that they had acquired someone else's identity. They might not feel that they look like themselves, at least at the beginning; but that is not the same thing as feeling that they look like someone else. For in any case, large though the part played by appearance is, it is not the whole story about identity, in which memory, character traits, likes and dislikes, and location in a web of relationships, are vitally important too.

Early in the debate about face transplants a victim of Crouzon's Syndrome was asked what she thought about the possibility of having one. She said she would have one as soon as they became available, because the gross distortions of face and cranium caused by her genetic disorder meant that she was born with no eye sockets, and with her teeth in her sinus cavities. She had had to undergo dozens of operations to get a less abnormal appearance, merely to be able to 'face the world' – the exactly appropriate phrase in the circumstances.

The redoubtable Simon Weston, by contrast, who was badly burned on HMS *Sir Galahad* during the Falklands conflict, and had to have over seventy operations on his scarred face and body, said that he would not choose to have a face transplant, although (as a member of the ethics committee on face transplants at the Royal Free Hospital in London) he would not stop others having them if reconstructive work proved unsatisfactory. His reason is that he has grown used to his rebuilt face, and wears his scars with honour.

As this shows, personal decision would play a large factor in future face transplants, and the fact that the subjects of them chose to have them would make a difference to how well they adapted afterwards. It is hard for those who really need, or would strongly like to have, a face transplant to be told by people of normal appearance what all the drawbacks might be, and for ethics committees to prevaricate because of the difficulties they expect others to suffer. That is often the way with medical advances; they are held up by caution, sometimes appropriate and sometimes the result of uncertainty, while those who are prepared to take the plunge are impotently forced to wait.

The success or otherwise of face transplants will of course depend in the end on how well medical management of the physiological mechanics of transplantation develops, and on the quality of the psychological support that recipients give themselves or get from others. Now that face transplants have arrived they are here to stay; and for the reason given earlier about quality-of-life being life itself, on the whole they are a good thing.

Faith schools

Just two words state the objection to faith-based schools: 'Northern Ireland'. The segregation of Catholic and Protestant school-children has been one of the major causes and sustainers of inter-community tensions in that troubled region. Why have the bitter lessons thus taught not been learned?

Some people offer just a one-word objection to religion-based education: 'madrassahs'. Madrassahs are not automatically terrorist breeding grounds, and most are surely not, but they equally surely can be. Some of Pakistan's madrassahs were Taliban and Al Qaeda factories, which we know because during Afghanistan's war with Russia the United States funded some of them as resistance training grounds.

There are at least three reasons for finding faith-based schooling deeply objectionable. One is that it involves the indoctrination of intellectually defenceless children, and that is a form of abuse. It is no accident that over three-quarters of all faith schools in Britain are primary schools, for as the Jesuits said, 'Give me the child until age seven and I will give you the man.' A responsible curriculum would include a sociological survey of the different religions and their history, leaving pupils to make up their own minds much later whether they are going to believe any of them. Of course the faiths know that the numbers of their votaries would be drastically lowered by this means, since mature consideration of religious claims would persuade very few hitherto unbiased minds. This is precisely why the faiths are so eager to indoctrinate their own children in segregated schools.

The second reason is that although the various faiths currently make common cause in demanding tax-payer support for their schools, and legal protection from criticism or opposition, the inevitability is that since the different faiths intrinsically blaspheme one another, the result of religiously segregated education can only be eventual tensions. A far safer route to national cohesion is secular schooling in which children of all communities are taught together. If their parents wish to subject them to religious instruction they can do it after school hours, or in private schools for which they pay out of their own pockets.

This connects with the third point. Tax-payer's money – my atheist's tax money included – should emphatically not go to support schooling premised on religious beliefs. Religion is a private matter of choice, and it is a profound injustice to force those who disagree with it to pay for children to be indoctrinated in it. At very most, if our society is going to tolerate the segregated indoctrination of small children into a religious ideology, it should be at their own parents' expense.

The government supports faith-based education in order to conciliate religious minorities, and because it hopes better behaved children will result. Its motives are worthy, but its logic is deeply flawed. Is it too late for them to undo the harm already begun?

Fox-hunting

A society shows its vigour when it argues with itself over its attitudes and practices, and never more so than when it succeeds in translating changes in the former into changes in the latter – providing, of course, that both are well justified.

This is exemplified by the case of British attitudes to animals and their treatment. An evolution of social sentiment resulted in the outlawing of bear-baiting and cock-fighting, in each case after long campaigns. John Wesley opposed all cruel sports (including fox-hunting) in the eighteenth century, but it was only in 1849 that cock-fighting was at last outlawed, and only now – over one hundred and fifty years later! – that fox-hunting has followed suit.

Now that hunting with hounds is banned, animal welfare campaigners can claim success in their long struggle to persuade society against tolerating cruel sports premised on the suffering and death of animals. But for those whose livelihoods and passions are deeply involved in hunting with hounds, the ban is more than a bitter blow, it is a devastating one; to such an extent that despite the unequivocal fact that a large majority of people in the country and in Parliament were no longer prepared to tolerate their sport, the proponents of fox-hunting defied democracy by opposing the ban both legally and illegally.

In all the angry exchanges that surrounded the issue, an important point has been neglected. This is that there is no need for hunting kennels and stables to be closed, for hounds to be put down, or for huntsmen to lose their jobs. On the contrary, there is an opportunity waiting to be grasped here which could secure and enhance the hunting world.

The opportunity lies in hunts switching to drag-hunting and 'bloodhounding', and perhaps even doing so competitively, with the Quorn, the North Cotswold, the Old Berkshire, the South Devon Foxhounds, the Beaufort, the Wynnstay, and others, competing to see which of them can find the drag fastest, perhaps riding over the same or similar terrain after a drag scent laid by an expert countryman with an eye for a good ride.

This last point has a significant implication. When Trollope celebrated the glories of the hunt in many of his novels, what he hymned was the joy of the gallop across open fields, the fresh air, the challenges posed by hedges and ditches, muddy lanes and woodland trees, comradeship, and the exhilaration of the encounter between human, horse and nature. If this is what matters most, and not any malign pleasure at the sight of an exhausted animal being torn to death by hounds, then there can be no objection to a skilfully laid drag.

One can imagine the livelihood of grooms and kennelmen being enhanced by revenue from television coverage of drag-hunting competitions. One can imagine some in the hunting community becoming celebrated dragsmen, laying courses that give excellent sport so that hunts can compete against dragsmen as well as each other. Once hunting with hounds has ceased to be a blood sport, it might – given the skill, excitement and panache involved – become even more of a spectator sport, with all that this implies for the rural economy.

Suggest this to hunting folk, though, and they turn up their noses at it. A drag can never have the unpredictability of the 'real thing', they say, for the real thing is a chase whereas drag is a follow; and they find a world of difference there. In fact these objections can be met by making the drag a chase, as happens in 'bloodhounding', where the hounds follow a running man rather than a laid scent. But the scent could be dragged from a running horse, reintroducing the chase element, and allowing the view halloo.

There are many successful drag-hunts around the country – the North East Cheshire, Jersey, the New Forest, and others. Though requiring larger areas than a fox-hunt, they offer a number of significant advantages. Advance permission can be secured from farmers for the route, preventing the annoyance and damage farmers often suffer. Hunts of graded difficulty can be devised for people of different equestrian skills, which means that many more people could take up riding to hounds; which again means that the sport could offer serious commercial opportunities, enhancing the rural economy and protecting the traditions and livelihoods of people who work in it.

In short, if hunting folk will use their imaginations and see an opportunity rather than a tragedy in the hunting ban, much good might result from it. As Sun Tzu said, 'One opportunity grasped is a dozen opportunities made.' Instead of fighting the inevitable, let hunters see what they already have as an investment and let them use it to hunt a dozen new opportunities for themselves.

God and the European Constitution

Some of the European Union's Catholic countries (most of them new members) supported the Pope in his efforts to have a reference to the continent's religious past included in the preamble of the EU constitution. There are good reasons why he and they did not succeed. The most important is that the social, political and material development of Europe since the beginning of modern times in the seventeenth century is the result of a hard-fought process by which the European intellect freed itself from the hegemony of religious belief, thereby establishing secularism – the separation of Church and state – which has been the single largest factor in Europe's progress ever since.

The liberating forces were the scientific revolution and the Enlightenment. They jointly transformed the world, overwhelmingly for the good. The technologies we live by, from computers to medical treatments, arc testaments to the genius of science. The rule of law, democracy, civil liberties and general education are testaments to Enlightenment principles. The improvement they have effected in the quality of human life has at times been intermitted, it is true, either by opposition to them (as in the Counter-Enlightenment) or misapplications of them (as in the diversion of science to production of increasingly destructive weapons); but the worst that was done in these respects has never halted the flow of benefits they brought.

Yet the respective contributions of science and Enlightenment to improving the human condition, and especially to liberating individuals from the slaveries of ignorance, poverty and super-stition, was opposed at every step by religious reaction, and they took place against a background of long and bitter religious wars and persecutions. The grip of long-ossified belief had to be prised away finger by stiff finger, and the task remains incomplete; but most Europeans now live in secular democracies, protected by law, equipped with at least a usable basic level of education, and free to make up their own minds, as their consciences dictate, on whether or not to accept a religious faith.

It is a rich irony therefore for the Church to try to insinuate reference to its beliefs into a document which is both an outcome and an expression of the long difficult struggle that Europe waged to free itself from the influence of religion over both public and private life, and the profound conflicts thus caused.

Supporters of the Pope's proposal set store by the fact that Christianity is a major part of the European tradition. Cynics might say that there are many aspects of the European tradition – two less happy examples among them are witch-burning and fascism – that we would do better to forget; which reminds us that something being part of Europe's heritage is not by itself a reason for celebrating it. And where the balance between posi-tive and negative legacies is questionable, there is good reason for reticence, as for example with colonialism. The same applies to Europe's religious past, for which some of Raphael's paintings and Bach's music are only part-compensations for the centuries of immense suffering in wars and persecutions that religion brought.

Votaries of religions are wise if they recognise that secu-larism's disinterest towards them, so long as they are peaceful, provides an assurance of survival; for a non-secular state would by definition privilege one faith over others, with the danger that this would outlaw rivals as heresies, and persecute them. But where religions are a matter of private credulity, and the state tolerates them as such, intervening only when they cause public harm or when their practices violate human rights (as with female circumcision, for example, or if some zealot revived human sacrifice), everyone benefits.

Blunt criticism of religion's pretensions to be taken seriously in twenty-first-century Europe might focus on two further matters. The first is that religion is, frankly understood, organised superstition; and superstition is the residuum of mankind's infancy, when the forces of nature were personalised in a rudimentary effort to understand and control them. Then gods were pictured as invisible kings, living on mountains or in the sea, responsible for thunder, earthquakes, and everything else inexplicable. As the human mind matured, religion became sophisticated in self-defence, dressing its primitive origins in the elaborations of theology, and dignifying its practices with great buildings and rich vestments. This latter is not true of fundamentalist versions, of course, but then their constituencies differ little in mindset from the first believers, for whom a streak of lightning was a spear thrown from the clouds.

In contemporary Europe we should not continue to indulge the descendants of these early superstitions, but should instead be liberating minds, especially those of the young. This is especially important given that almost all the major conflicts in history, as in the world today, are the product, direct or by legacy, of differences in religious dogma and practice. No one has ever fought a war because of disagreements in geology or botany; but humanity has bled to death over the question of whether a wafer of bread becomes human flesh when a priest whispers incantations over it. This stark contrast needs to be taken seriously; for until it is, we condemn ourselves to repeat the futile quarrels of the past.

The second point is that everywhere religion flourishes,

backwardness flourishes too: in educational, economic and political respects. This is no surprise. Until very recently – literally, the last few decades – the parts of Europe where Catholicism retained a dominant presence were poor and benighted as a result, and the scene of an immense violation of human rights in the form of the enslavement of women to constantly repeated pregnancies and imprisonment in marriage. Elsewhere in the world where human lives labour under religious hegemony, this lesson remains dangerously visible.

Defenders of religion believe that without it humanity would lose a grip on two treasures: morality and spirituality. This belief is a measure of the extraordinary success the Church has had in making us forget that traditions of thought far richer than its own exist to teach us about both: two and a half thousand years of philosophy, the arts and literature, overflowing with insight and instruction into the deepest and most beautiful possibilities for human life, little of it depending on belief in Zeus or Osiris, Brahman or Baal. Indeed, superstition has been a barrier to our benefiting from this wealth: only the free mind has a chance to do so, though happily that wealth itself is the resource for helping the mind to become so.

In the light of such reflections, the idea of incorporating reference to religion, which Europe has fought so hard and long to liberate itself from, in the wording of its new constitution, is unacceptable. Let those who accept a religion observe it privately, but let them not impose it on the rest of us.

Humanism and religion

A rose might indeed smell as sweet by any other name, but names matter nevertheless, and it especially matters that the terms 'humanism' and 'religion' should have clear definitions so that the temptation to describe the former as a species of the latter can be scrupulously avoided. Some succumb to this badly mistaken temptation because they wish humanism would be a movement with a credo that would sustain the formation of communities of like-minded folk, who can hold mutually supportive meetings and the like – making it a substitute for membership of a congregation of the faithful in one or another faith. But humanism is not such a thing, and religion is a quite different thing.

Humanism is a general outlook based on two allied premises, which allow considerable latitude to what follows from them. The premises are, first, that there are no supernatural entities or agencies in the universe, and second, that our individual and social ethics must be drawn from, and responsive to, facts about the nature and circumstances of human beings. Humanism, in other words, starts from the fact that human beings exist in an entirely natural universe, and that the human good must be shaped accordingly. There can be much debate about what the human good can and should be, ranging from philosophical abstractions to the politics of the hustings; but it is distinctively humanist only if it eschews efforts to decide these matters by expressly invoking the idea that there are supernatural powers in the world whose purposes and desires dictate what the human good is to be.

Religion, by contrast, is expressly premised on belief in the existence of supernatural agencies, and moreover ones that in some way matter to the human good. In typical cases of religion it is supposed that the supernatural agencies have a personal interest in the obedience or conformity of human beings to their purposes; and such religions further suppose that human petition or blandishment can alter the supernatural purposes in question, chiefly in the form of prayer and sacrifice, the latter ranging from lit candles and novenas to the slit throats of sacrificial victims. But unless an outlook premises the existence and (usually) interest of supernatural beings, and demands belief in and a response to their existence, it is not a religion and should not be called one.

Neither Buddhism in its original Theravada form, nor Confucianism, are therefore religions; they are atheistic in the quite literal sense of this term. (Do not be misled by the Chinese use of the notion of 'tian' into trying to interpret it otherwise.) They are philosophies. This applies also to Stoicism, for half a millennium before Constantine the outlook of most educated people in the classical world. The Stoics had a notion of reason (the 'logos') as the ordering principle of the world, which those anxious to impute theistic leanings to them interpret as a deity in the Judaeo-Christian-Islamic sense. But it was no such thing; it was a principle of rational structure, of rightness and fittingness in the natural order, to which ethical endeavour – so they argued – should fit itself. The Stoics did not 'worship' it, petition it or expect it to change its mind about something in response to a lit candle – in short, they did not think of it as a person or as conscious or purposive in any way. And these things it would have had to be to qualify as a deity, and the service of it as a religion.

The theatre and ritual of religion – the Mass, communal prayer, weddings, funerals and the like – answer a need many people have for communal celebrations of significant moments in life and death. Humanist groups can offer non-religious versions of some of these observances for those who do not construct their own way of joining with friends and family to effect them. But it is a failure of imagination not to see that when people go to art galleries or concerts, or enjoy gardening or country walks, or get together in the pub or round the dinner table with friends, that they are in different ways expressing themselves aesthetically and socially in the same (and arguably better) way as people who band together in congregations. When illiterate peasants gathered from their dispersed farms in church every Sunday they had a dose of communality, theatre, and art (in the form of graphic and highly-coloured murals relating the New Testament story and the punishment they would receive if they disobeyed their priest's injunctions) art. Human resources have expanded since, and people can choose their own ways of satisfying the needs once met by that strict and propagandistic ration.

Humanism, though, is not even a philosophy, for it has no teachings beyond its two minimal premises, and obliges us to do nothing other than think for ourselves. Since it does not constitute a body of doctrine, a sequence of arguments, an adumbration of principles, or a code of living, and requires no belief in anything beyond what empirical evidence defeasibly and revisably requires, it is as far from being a religion as anything could be, for a religion is all these things and more.

Religious folk try to turn the tables on people of a naturalistic and humanistic outlook by charging them with 'faith' in science or 'faith' in reason. Faith, they seem to have forgotten, is what you have *in the face of* facts and reason; the point of the Doubting Thomas story, remember, is that it is more blessed to believe without evidence than with it, and Kierkegaard was not the first to welcome the very absurdity of what faith requires in the way of belief, since it thereby makes faith all the more a leap of will.

No such thing is required to 'believe in' science or reason. Science is always open to challenge and refutation, faith is not; reason must be rigorously tested by its own lights, faith rejoices in unreason. Once again, a humanistic outlook is as far from sharing the characteristics of religion as it can be. By definition, in short, humanism is not religion, any more than religion is or can be a form of humanism.

Precept and example

Is it better to teach by precept or by example? A paradox infects the first method, and a problem infects the second. The paradox in the first is that only the wise can learn from precepts, but, being already wise, they do not need them. The problem in the second is that example is a hit-and-miss teacher; some see the point, others do not, and yet others see it well enough, but do not like it.

These reflections are prompted by the fact that the United States is currently engaged in teaching democracy to the rest of the world by precept, but not by example. On the contrary, the dismaying spectacle of presidential and congressional elections stained by slur and smear, whose participants need millions of dollars just to get near the starting post, where serious doubts attend the electoral process – fraud-prone electronic ballots, deliberately abbreviated electoral rolls, emotion-directed advertising – and where more than half the electorate fail to take part, is scarcely a shining example of democracy at work. The main lesson it teaches is how to preserve the status quo; the point is neatly captured by Gore Vidal's remark that the US is governed by a single political party with two right wings.

The United States is in fact a plutocracy, a polity in which wealth is the basis of power. At current values it takes a hundred million dollars to be elected (cynics would say: to purchase the office of) President of the United States. The campaign which raises the most money has the best chance of winning, because money means advertisements, mobility for the candidate and his (*sic*) staff, leaflets, flags, razzmatazz, lobbyists, research, polling and all the rest of the expensive business of trying to win. In fact this price-tag is considerably too low, because running for President is a life-long task in which many further costs have to be paid, and not just in cash, to get into the right position even for a chance of nomination.

Theoretically, a democracy is a political entity in which anyone should be able to stand for election simply on the basis of his or her attributes and ideas. But even in Britain elections cost millions, from the deposit each candidate must put down in order to stand in a constituency, to the advertising costs involved in putting across one's own message and inflicting damage on the opposing message.

In ancient Athens the qualification for office was eloquence. At first blush this seems a questionable aptitude; do we not have plenty of mistrustworthy examples – the glib and oleaginous politician, the fast-talker, the smoothie, the snake-oil salesman? It is true that when antiquity's Sophists set to work, teaching anyone who could afford the fee 'how to make the worse case seem the better' as one of them put it – thus inventing 'spin' – the persuasive tongue began to seem a disingenuous thing.

But the reason that Sophists could sell the art of eloquence at all was that in the pristine state of the ancient polities, eloquence was a mark of intelligence, knowledge, experience and good judgement. These qualities by themselves make anyone eloquent; they speak with the tongue of nature. No one thus equipped need learn the tropes of rhetoric or the psychology of persuasion, still less the power of the calculated witticism and the covert insult.

Despite claiming the name, the ancient Greek democracies were anything but: slaves, women and men under thirty, between them constituting the vast majority in each state, were voiceless. Among the enfranchised remainder, such dif-ferentiating factors as reputation and personality might work their magic, but it was only later in the Greek city-state's history that family name, wealth and the ossification of institutions leached power from the 'agora' (the forum, the open space where the men of the state gathered to debate) and put it into the hands of those with a knack for manipulation.

Among the drawbacks of the democracy of eloquence was the fact that there was no guarantee that the most persuasive speech contained the best advice. But the Athenian agora was not an assembly of fools: very often what made a speech the most persuasive was precisely that it contained the best advice, and the listeners knew it when they heard it.

It is not clear, in short, that the money and calumny of our modern hustings serve us better.

Private China

There is a Chinese saying which runs, 'Above, there is heaven; below, there is Hangzhou and Suzhou.' It is intended to convey the legendary beauty of these two Yangtze Delta cities, Hangzhou with its famous Western Lake and Suzhou with its canals and celebrated classical gardens. These last, bearing such romantic names as 'The Humble Administrator's Garden', 'The Master of the Fishing Nets Garden' and 'The Pavilion of the Waves', are mostly very small in area, but are made to seem large by cunning arrangements of twisting paths, each segment of which is hidden from the others by bamboo, dwarf trees, rocks of unusual texture and shape, and latticed walls. No doubt unintentionally, the garden designers of past dynasties thereby created a strikingly apt metaphor for Chinese society and government, not just in their own time but for the present too; for both Chinese society and government are mazes of hidden paths, secrets, deceiving prospects and tricks of perspective.

This reflection was prompted by news that China's State Council instructed the China Law Society to set up an 'information law study committee' to draft a Freedom of Information bill. According to reports, the committee presented a draft to the State Council in July 2002, but as a result of 'crucial questions' being raised by the 'public' (there is no independent confirmation that a public consultation exercise took place) the State Council sent the draft back to the committee, and nobody seems to know when a revised version will appear, nor therefore when or even if a Freedom of Information law will eventually follow. All that is known about the first draft is that it consisted of seven chapters comprising forty-two articles, a precise enough piece of information to make the reports appear plausible.

To the untutored eye the fact that the Party leaders in their Forbidden City enclave are even considering a Freedom of Information law looks like a sea-change. Optimists could see it as an aspect of China's efforts to conform to global norms on transparency and the rule of law, chiefly in the interests of inward investment by companies attracted by the potentially huge market for their goods, but hesitant because of corruption and China's skewed and still patchy legal system. But the probability is that 'Freedom of Information' in the Chinese context is in fact Newspeak for precisely the opposite, namely, a law aimed at increasing control over access to information now that the new communications technologies are making China far more internally and externally porous to information, not a little of it disagreeable to the Chinese government: chiefly satellite broadcasting, and the internet and e-mail, both of the latter now accessible via mobile telephony.

But although the Chinese authorities make strenuous efforts to control the flow of information from these sources, in a quite different and specific sphere it is likely that they do indeed have the opposite aim. To explain this one needs to grasp that China's well-known culture of secrecy and manipulation of information, far antedating the regime which has been in place since 1949, so permeates society and government that ministerial departments, Provincial governments and the separate regional military commands not only all keep secrets from the outside world, but from one another too – and even from central government. The same is true, even further, between officers and personnel of the same ministry, military command or local authority. The reasons for this are many, but they include the insistent Chinese urge to make everything look as good as possible (thus hiding mistakes, poor figures, failures) not just to outsiders but even to one another; fear of criticism, or of the party leadership's displeasure; and jealousy and rivalries, not least between the different factions of the Party itself, which is multiply internally divided, although two broad groupings – a conservative and a modernising wing – collect most of the divisions.

This internal secrecy has played a large part in turning difficulties into disasters in China, most notably in connection with HIV/AIDS and SARS, and it is these two matters in particular that have prompted China's leadership to demand at last that provincial governments and different ministerial departments of the central government keep each other informed when such problems arise. They are not keen to break with tradition when it comes to the frequent industrial accidents and rural uprisings which, although censorship obscures most of them from public notice, are frequent in China, so local authorities are encouraged not to let the rest of the country know if, say, a power station has malfunctioned, or toxic waste has polluted a water supply. But the refusal all through the 1980s and early '90s to accept the HIV/AIDS problem meant that it has become greatly worse than it might have been; and the absurd failures surrounding the SARS outbreak, stemming from a blind refusal to acknowledge the existence of the problem in Guangdong Province in the first place, was responsible for the damage caused to health and economies far beyond China's borders.

In this respect, then, the proposed law probably aims to provide a framework for intra-governmental information control and exchange of the kind required for effective management of SARS-type crises. But, as is the way with governments of all stripes, the Chinese will unquestionably try to profit from the occasion by seeking to formalise constraints on 'undesirable' information being circulated inside China or coming into it from outside. They already do this by jamming transmissions, imposing internet filters, monitoring e-mails, and handing down harsh punishments to end-users. The most likely effect of any information law will therefore be to give the authorities the cosmetic advantage of legitimising what is *de facto* already the case. The law should accordingly be called 'The Party's Freedom to Control Information' law, for it is not likely to involve the chopping-down of bamboo screens along the winding paths of China's secret garden.

Science and faith before Darwin

One of mankind's more questionable talents is a reluctance to relinquish its old superstitions. Our earliest science took the form of belief in supernatural agencies, powerful and invisible, whose tread was heard in the clouds' thunder, and whose anger at the breaking of taboos expressed itself in earthquakes and plagues. Hence arose our earliest technologies – namely: sacrifice, prayer, fearful adherence to traditions of dress and diet thought to please the powers lurking beyond man's comprehension.

As these words were written in the early years of the twenty-first century, on a computer, by electric light, with a laser playing across the surface of a nearby compact disc to reproduce sounds of music, so the world awaited news, to be announced by smoke and bells, of the decision of a hundred or so elderly men concerning who will next legislate by fiat for the morals of millions. I refer of course to the cardinals in Rome, who were at that moment busy choosing a Pope. Halfway between them in the Vatican and this author here in the sceptred isle of Britain lay the most important physics laboratory in the world: the particle accelerator at CERN in Switzerland, where investigation of the fundamental structure and properties of matter is carried out.

What a contrast, eh? One would have thought that by now the intellectual dinosaurs of superstition would have slunk away to die of their own absurdity. It is a matter of sociological and historical interest to examine the reasons why that has not happened. The tale belongs chiefly to the epoch between the rise of science and Darwin's revolutionary impact on the world.

Everyone who reads is familiar with the story of Darwin and the reception of his theory of evolution by natural selection in the mid-nineteenth century, when the problem of the irreconcilability of science and religion came to a head. But like all things, the Darwinian crisis did not come out of nothing. From the mid-seventeenth century to Darwin's immediate predecessors, the period's best minds attempted to reconcile the increasingly divergent discoveries of science with scripture, or at least with the fundamentals of 'natural theology', culminating in the celebrated attempt by William Paley to prove the existence of God by means of the 'argument from design'.

The seventeenth- and eighteenth-century savants who wrestled with the conflict between evidence and reason, and the dictates of religious tradition, were mostly serious and principled men. They included Thomas Burnet, John Ray and James Hutton, who at the same time as contributing to the growth of science made every effort to reconcile their faith with the sharply contrasting truths of what their eyes and minds told them – not least about the age of the earth, the testimony of geology, the imperfection and amorality of a diverse natural realm, and much besides.

An intriguing theme in the tale is the connection between the best efforts of the faith-inclined naturalists and geologists and the eventual triumph of science. It is a connection that runs through 'natural theology', the effort to prove the existence and demonstrate the nature of a deity from the evidences supposed to be offered by the world itself. In Paley's version, the arrangement and intricacy of things in nature bespeaks a designer, just as a watch does; so the world itself is proof that there is a God. (It is remarkable how every proponent of the argument stops there, as if invoking a supposed but unexplained non-natural designer of nature explained anything at all.) If the world is designed by God, it must be good (another leap of faith rather than logic), therefore such things as diseases and tsunamis must be good; and with them the inequalities in fortunes and social status of human beings.

When he was a student Darwin read and admired Paley, and was persuaded by his arguments. His researches on the famous *Beagle* voyage taught him differently, though not without a fearful struggle of conscience, for he realised that what his scientific investigations had taught him meant the destruction of the cosy world-view offered by religion. He once said that he felt as if he had killed God. But it was in Paley's pages that Darwin first saw the importance of Malthus's theory of population, an idea that helped him to see how evolution worked. Many had hypothesised evolution before Darwin, including his own relation Erasmus Darwin, but none had seen the mechanism. This was Darwin's contribution – and Paley, arguing the very opposite case, helped him to see it.

The classic account of the monumental struggle between faith and reason as it played out in the lives of sincere individuals is of course Edmund Gosse's *Father and Son*. It is a story not quite yet done; what money and advertising can achieve is being tried by the proponents of so-called 'Intelligent Design' (a fig-leaf for Creationism) in the United States. To borrow a memorable remark made by Bernard Williams in another connection, 'Intelligent Design' theory is the tribute paid, in poor coin, by irrationality to reason; which one supposes is an advance, though a small one, on blind faith alone.

Sexually transmitted diseases

Human beings are infectious creatures. Public transport is responsible for most of the communicable respiratory diseases people suffer from, and if every hand that held a rail or strap in a bus left a bright blue trail of grease instead of an invisible one, and if the microbes crawling about in it were big enough to see, the buses would be empty in a second. Most colds are caught from handling objects other people handle, such as pens on counters at banks and supermarkets.

At the same time, the sharing of germs is what keeps us healthy; we inoculate one another, and strengthen one another's immune systems, by breathing over each other on the tube. If you lived in a sealed environment from birth until adulthood, then exposed yourself to the multitudes, you would be dead within days. This is what happened to many Africans and native Americans when European missionaries and conquistadors arrived among them.

Sexually transmitted diseases are in essence the product of the same circumstances as provide a disease vector in the public transport setting. If you were trying to be witty, you might call them 'pubic transport' diseases instead. What they share in common is their need for proximity, contact, closeness of human to human. Decency and morality is not offended by these circumstances when public transport is the setting; pubic transport – to labour the pun – has the moral majority (in truth, a vociferous moral minority) up in arms when the news tells us, as it frequently does, that rates of sexually transmitted disease (STD) have risen.

There is no question that STDs are a bad thing. Some are merely uncomfortable, some are deadly. A number threaten fertility. The course of the deadly STDs, chiefly AIDS and syphilis, is long and can take terrible forms. Even the treatable ones carry an aura of horror: gonorrhoea is an ugly word, and evokes images of Daumier-like nastiness. Some of the non-life-threatening ones are incurable, such as herpes, and some of the absurd-sounding ones, like genital warts, can cause cancer of the cervix and penis.

These celibacy-inducing facts are rehearsed with Gothic relish by those who would limit sex to the Saturday night duties of hitherto inexperienced monogamous couples in the married state. Moreover, the fact that sex includes merely kissing and petting – both can transmit syphilis and AIDS, herpes, and some of the others – is used to dissuade the desirous from seeking even the simulacrum of passion.

More earnestly yet, STDs are invoked by the big hitters on the moral front as evidence of God's wrath, justly provoked by our sins. When syphilis assumed epidemic status in Europe at the end of the fifteenth century – allegedly brought back by Columbus and his crew from the New World, though it had been recorded by Hippocrates in ancient Greece, and studies of the remains at Pompeii show that some there had it too – the Church immediately said it was divine punishment, which added a burden to the sufferers, who in addition to the illness had to bear the disgust of the righteous, and a consequent lack of help.

That is what happened in America at the beginning of the AIDS crisis. Moral majoritarians again attributed it to the deity's displeasure, this time with the bath-house culture of New York and San Francisco, and their condemnation slowed the earliest efforts to find treatments and give help – recall that

Mr Reagan was in the White House for the first eight years of the crisis, and the moralists had his ear.

What distorts the picture and warps judgements here is the fact that sex is involved. STDs are transmitted by contact between people. But that applies to all communicable diseases, by definition. Sex is among the closest of human contacts, and therefore provides the most effective bridge for the diseases in question. But newspaper headlines do not bemoan the closeness of bus seats, or the fact that swimming pools exist (an excellent vector for hepatitis). Yet introduce sex into the picture, and all is shock-horror.

There is in fact a circumstance in which people are closer, and share more bugs, even than in sex – and that is ordinary family life. Moralists approve of ordinary family life. This shows that they do not mind closeness, and the exchange of viruses and microbes, just providing that there is no sex involved. I suspect they might be prepared to go further and say: providing there is no pleasure involved.

The moral of this story is not a moralising one, but one wholly about hygiene. Cleanliness, condoms and common sense are the answer, together with support for the scientific research that will prevent or cure the penalty for ignoring any of the three.

The responsibilities
of the writer

It is unfashionable to talk about responsibilities in this age of rights, even though responsibilities and rights are often the same thing seen from opposite sides. Talk of rights carries with it encouraging connotations of litigation initiated and damages won, whereas mention of duty and responsibility only makes us think of our Victorian great-grandparents; for we think, more rightly than not, that, like thick folds of black Sunday gabardine, their sanctimonious talk of duty muffled the joy in things, and sucked the light out of living.

Such talk doubtless had that effect because it was prompted by the religiosity characteristic of the age. But it therefore gave responsibility an undeservedly bad name. It made responsibility seem worthy, earnest, dead-handed and grudging, whereas in truth it is crisp and sharp, with a citrus tang; for once one recognises a responsibility in some connection, one is clear about what to do – a boon in a world otherwise leaden with ambiguities and uncertainty.

Like everyone else in every walk of life, writers have responsibilities. But they are not responsibilities of a worthy and dismal stamp. Writers have no responsibility to inculcate good morals or good manners in anyone, or to take any government's side, or to tell the truth, further a cause, spare blushes, pretend that the world is at least as full of ripeness as rottenness, or any other such thing.

But they do have responsibilities to themselves, and to the language they write in. They might arguably not have a responsibility to entertain (though they are wise to), but at least they have a responsibility not to bore. They also have a responsibility not to obfuscate, and that includes not writing in unsolvable riddles in order to appear deep or clever. (A place will be reserved in the deepest circle of hell for academics on this score.) If they have no responsibility to tell the truth, they certainly have a responsibility to tell a truth as they see it. And they certainly have a responsibility not to lie.

Some of these claims merit expansion. The first – that writers have responsibilities to themselves – especially requires clarification. I do not mean that writers are obliged to accept suffering for their art, by going hungry, thirsty and cold for it, or by trying to enjoy their failures. I mean that they should endeavour to get good advances, that they should make sure to go on holiday in the sun regularly, and that they should enjoy the freebies in the green room at literary festivals. In short and generally, they have a responsibility to grasp what is going with grateful hands, so that the muse within can be fat, oiled and well supplied for its labours. For, as the saying has it, how can he do good for others who is not good to himself?

The second – responsibility to the language – surely speaks for itself. No one can disagree that lazy, sloppy, weak, loose, cheap, used, soiled, second-hand, flat, unclear, illogical and ungrammatical language, or anything that even faintly smells of any of these things, is among other crimes irresponsible.

Not even writers of advertising copy and public signs and notices are exempt from this stricture. To use the example cited earlier in the essay on language purity, think about this sentence, seen in a bus, bringing to a close a notice to passengers concerning changes in routing and timing of a service: 'So the buses run smoother, and there are less delays.' According to the Murdoch (that is Rupert Murdoch) Professor of Linguistics at

Oxford University (yes, there is such a thing), this sentence is an acceptable example of how language naturally and inevitably changes despite the huffing and puffing of purists. Well, of course languages change, ineluctably so, though it is not illogical to mourn the fact sometimes, since the change is generally in the direction of lazy kinds of simplification, with the loss of such distinctions as between (for example) 'less' and 'fewer'. So there is no repining over the fact. But the point about 'the buses run smoother' is not language change, but logic. For this sentence implies that the buses have had new suspension fitted, resulting in fewer bumps ('less bumps', the inevitable sign might say, to keep company with 'less delays'), whereas in fact it is intended to mean that the bus services run more smoothly, the key lying in the difference between a comparative adjective applied to 'buses' and a comparative adverb applied to 'run'.

Perhaps what this means is that writers have a responsibility to do Latin at school.

Writers do not have a responsibility to make their paragraphs short (see the one before last) or long (see the one before this), nor even to make their sentences short, so long as clarity of sense is retained, and with it the interest of the reader; for although short sharp sentences are great supporters of clarity, and have their special uses in making points pungently and aiding the build-up of suspense in thriller novels, they can sometimes interfere with that prose virtue much admired and exploited by Lytton Strachey, namely, sequentiality – by which he meant the flow of meaning in a passage, the unfolding, mounting, accumulating, broadening path of information and imagery that takes the reader from a point lower in the scale of things to one very much higher, all the while held aloft on strong wings of sentence structure, constituted by a scaffolding of clauses, subclauses, suitable punctuation and what might be called 'mental breathings', these being minor caesurae in the flow allowing the reader to gather himself or herself before continuing to mount the escalier of artfully dovetailed phrases until the view from the top is achieved – as I hope it now is. Henry James and Immanuel Kant vie for top place in this art.

Poets are not alone in having a responsibility to keep the language fresh and alive. A glance over the landscape of our literature will reveal a remarkable truth: that almost any writing, on any subject, will survive and have its admirers if it is very good of its kind. To fell forests and clog up bookshelves with pages of ordinariness is not a responsible act. Of all the writer's responsibilities, therefore, this is clearly and obviously the greatest.

And after all it might be said that the discharge of this responsibility takes care of all the others mentioned above: not to bore, not to obfuscate, not to lie (bad writing can pervert even the truth by making it rebarbative to the taste of a reader), and to convey something honest from the writer's own perception of things.

Ah, the reader, just mentioned: and surely the writer has responsibilities to readers. As you would expect a philosopher to say, the answer to this is: yes and no. The Yes answer is amply catered for in all the foregoing on the writer's responsibility to self and language. The No answer applies to the fact that readers have responsibilities too, and it is not up to writers to do absolutely all the readers' work for them. Emerson said that we should give new acquaintances at least what we give a painting, namely, the advantage of a good light; and this is certainly what readers should be required to offer any book they open. But they also have to read intelligently, mindfully, responsively. La Rochefoucauld acidly observed that if an ass peers into a looking-glass he cannot expect an angel to look back; just so with readers, who will not find much in a book if they have brought nothing to it.

Of course this does not excuse the writer from the responsibility to avoid being boring and obscure. Readers are within their rights to toss such stuff into the rubbish bin, if they are sure it is not their own dimness that casts its shadows on the page. In short, a book is somewhat like a tango, which takes two; and both parties must be expected to play their part.

This is not, by the way, to subscribe to the absurd theory that books are written by their readers, and that we commit the 'intentional fallacy' if we think that the writer meant to say something and tried his or her damnedest to say it well. The vast slackening of human intellect called, for shorthand, 'post-modernism' has no part in this debate.

If any of the writerly responsibilities listed above can be singled out as closest in importance to the obvious one of doing the job well, it is implied in the 'grateful hands' remark: namely, that a writer should enjoy being one, and should accept the attendant profits and perks, if any such come, with relish.

The role of the intellectual

Ideas are the motors of history. They take many forms and have many sources, and often assume a life of their own, and prove to be bigger than the epochs they influence. As such they are matters of vital concern; and therefore it is necessary that they be examined and debated, glorified and criticised, adopted when good and defeated when bad. The job of doing these things belongs to all of us, but in practice it falls to those with a particular interest in, and sometimes aptitude for, the task. Such are the 'intellectuals'.

Intellectuals are people who are not just interested in ideas, but who actively engage with them. They set themselves the task – some of them see it as a duty, given the opportunities they have had for acquiring the relevant interests and skills – to analyse, to ask questions, to clarify, to seek fresh perspectives, to suggest, to criticise, to challenge, to complain, to examine and propose, to debate, to educate, to comment, to suggest and, where possible, to discover. They see it as part of their remit to contribute to the conversation society has with itself about matters moral, political, educational and cultural, and to remind society of the lessons history taught it, and of the promises it has made for its future. And thereby the intellectual comes sometimes to be – as Socrates elected himself to be – a gadfly on the body politic, stinging it into alertness of mind.

The risk run by intellectuals is to seem pretentious, fatuous, pompous, self-congratulatory and given to polysyllabic mouthings of banality and cliché. And too often they actually are so – often enough to have a bad name in the Anglo-Saxon world, where blunt common sense is valued above Gauloise-wreathed nuances of gossip about concepts.

But the advantage to society of energetic intellectual activity is that it offers society self-awareness, wakefulness and clarity, inspiration and new ideas, and intelligence in debate and action. A sluggard community which never asks questions or inspects the world around it with a bright eye, and which never tries out different ways of understanding its circumstances, is sure first to stagnate, and then to slip backwards.

Thus do intellectuals perform a service: by keeping the hope of progress alive, and by never ceasing to argue about its nature and direction.

'Third World Literature'

Some years ago the literary theorist and Urdu poet Aijaz Ahmad engaged in a celebrated controversy with the American critic Frederic Jameson over the question of 'Third World Literature'. Jameson had eloquently advocated a widening of the literature syllabus in American academies to include works from outside the standard list of Western classics. Ahmad welcomed Jameson's call, but was deeply disturbed to find him talking of 'Third World Literature' as if it were a homogeneous category. There is, Ahmad argues, no such category: there are instead the many diverse literatures of many different countries which for reasons of geopolitical theory tend too glibly to be lumped together as 'the Third World'.

In Ahmad's view, the 'metropolitan' (First World, Western) propensity to think in agglomerative terms of 'Third World Culture' generates a false understanding of recent world history and the way literature relates to it. The story goes as follows. In the three decades following 1945 nationalism was a powerful force in African and Asian countries engaged in throwing off colonial bonds. Literary theorists applauded the drive to cultural independence associated with these anti-colonial struggles; but in doing so subsumed them all under the single 'Third World' label. But with the rise of post-structuralist literary theories in the 1970s nationalism itself came to be seen as oppressive, coercive and retrograde. According to post-structuralism, it is nonsensical to think in terms of such concepts as the origin of national identity and the possession of collective cultural consciousness; and it is likewise mistaken to interpret the development of these phenomena by means of determinate historical narratives. There are only individuals, post-structuralists argue, each with his own relative point of view; and there is no independent rationality or historical truth by whose means sense can be made of national struggles and the fate of cultures.

Ahmad is opposed both to 'Third-Worldism' and to post-structuralism. His chief reason is that, despite the fact that the political, economic and historical analyses offered by Marxism appear to have been exploded by events, he remains a Marxist nonetheless; and as such believes that, although nationalism has too often suppressed questions of 'gender' and class, and has too often been retrogressive, it nevertheless has progressive forms, and these must be historically understood.

If fellow critics try to dismiss Ahmad's views on the grounds that the moths of history have eaten his theoretical garb bare, they will be doing him an injustice. Marxist theory may be in eclipse, but on this occasion it serves as a powerful dissenting voice to the two orthodoxies – 'Third-Worldism' and post-structuralism – which have succeeded each other in misrepresenting, as Ahmad convincingly shows, the nature of the many different literatures and cultures flourishing in Africa and Asia. Because of this vigorously argued claim, Ahmad's voice is one of the most important in the current critical debate.

One of the best features of Ahmad's account is its disentangling of geopolitical appearances from cultural realities. At the Bandung Conference in Indonesia in 1955, presided over by the formidable figures of Nehru and Zhou En Lai, an effort was made to forge a consensus among nations outside the immediate hegemonies of the United States and Soviet Union. Writers like Edward Said have mythologised this moment as the birth of the Third World; but Ahmad shows that, for all its importance otherwise, Bandung does not mark – for nothing could ever mark – the creation of that 'Third World Culture' which metropolitan criticism, addressing itself to a phantom of its own making, so vociferously praised and then later attacked.

It is a great pity that Ahmad will not be read by the general educated public, but only by fellow theorists. If he addressed himself to readers outside academic circles he would spread more widely his message concerning the crudity and complacency of Western thinking about what lies beyond its cultural borders. In the newly emerging world such understanding is essential, its absence a danger – and sometimes a terrible one.

PEOPLE

Charles Darwin

C harles Darwin is a more important figure than any other
seminal thinker of the last two centuries – including Marx
and Freud – because his work has effected a more radical change
in human self-perception than anything before it in recorded
history, and the consequences of it are still, and with increasing
significance, infusing themselves into the life of mankind
through the biological sciences, most notably in the form of
genetic medicine.

Summarily put, before the Darwinian revolution we thought
of ourselves as special beings, occupying the summit of a div-
inely planned creation. After Darwin our perspective changed
utterly. Life, he taught us, is the product of long, slow, blind
struggles for survival, taking place over aeons. The prior belief
that the world was created on a Sunday morning four millennia
ago put mankind (especially white European mankind) at the
top – and not just figuratively speaking – of the tree of nature.
Try to imagine what it felt like to be assured of the truth of this
proposition; among many other things it explains the long-
standing sources of racism, colonialism, sexism, speciesism and
a host of other 'isms' that have bedevilled human history and
now seem intolerable.

But when humans see themselves as an evolving part of a
long and tortuous natural history, as apes who descended from
the top of a real tree, intimately close to other mammals and
behaving just like them in conflicts over resources and territory,
they no longer have grounds for the same superior opinion of

themselves. From the point of view of ruling hierarchies, the implied threat to religion is even worse, because nothing has ever been so effective in controlling people than their belief that an invisible super-policeman is watching them everywhere and always. ('Religion is false,' said Plato, 'but the masses should be encouraged to believe it; it keeps them in order.') Darwin's views exploded all that.

The oddity is that Darwin's revolution would have happened even if there had been no Darwin. He was the right man in the right place at the crucial time; his gifts as an observer and reasoner were by no means incidental to the shape that evolutionary theory took, but if he had not sailed round the world on the *Beagle*, someone else in the scientific circles of the day would, sooner rather than later, have brought those same ideas to light. Alfred Russel Wallace was hard on his heels.

To say this is neither to belittle Darwin's achievement, nor to reduce the enigma of his character. After the *Beagle* voyage collecting the data that prompted his version of evolutionary theory, Darwin waited and fretted many years before publishing it. The facts he had observed and studied plainly indicated evolution, yet to Darwin it felt – as he put it himself – as if by publicising the theory he was 'murdering God'. When at last *The Origin of Species* appeared he found, as he had guessed, that many others shared that view, and a violent controversy flared. Darwin was ill for much of his life – a tropical illness acquired on the voyage, or anxiety? – and shunned both publicity and conflict. He left the task of championing his views to such redoubtable allies as T. H. Huxley, who easily rebutted criticism from Bishop 'Soapy Sam' Wilberforce and others. But Darwin's theory hardly needed such help; it was its own defence, and it completely redrew mankind's intellectual map.

Ever since then Charles Darwin has been the centre of an industry. Books about him proliferate, and in publishing terms his own works, especially the classic *Origin of Species*, have begun to look biblical; they have been reprinted hundreds of times and translated into dozens of languages. His special contribution was to have found the mechanism by which evolution occurs: natural selection, operating through the reproductive success of organisms whose random mutations prove best-adapted to their environment. Subsequent research has extended and refined the picture he drew, even in the process of drawing powerful inferences from it. The rest is – unfolding, and burgeoning – history.

Henry Fielding

Henry Fielding had a mixed press in his own century. Sir John Hawkins attacked his *Tom Jones* as a book 'seemingly intended to sap the foundation of that morality which it is the duty of parents and all public instructors to inculcate in the minds of young people', and Dr Johnson, despite his own tenderness for the bosoms visible in the dressing-rooms of Garrick's theatre, described it as 'vicious'. But Edward Gibbon, pointing out that Fielding was a scion of the English branch of the Hapsburg family, claimed that, long after the Emperors were forgotten, Fielding's work would live on.

The philosopher Bernard Harrison has described Fielding's outlook as 'a morality of good-heartedness'. This emotion is described by Fielding as 'that benevolent and amiable Temper of Mind which disposes us to feel the Misfortunes and enjoy the Happiness of others; and consequently pushes us on to promote the latter, and prevent the former; and that without any abstract Contemplation of the Beauty of Virtue, and without the Allurement or Terrors of Religion'.

The whole of *Tom Jones* is a demonstration of this rational, optimistic and very eighteenth-century principle. But Fielding's first and clearest statement of the idea occurs in the too-neglected work in which his comic genius found itself, and which, in the figure of Parson Adams, contains one of the most endearing characters in English literature: *Joseph Andrews*.

Fielding wrote it as a satirical response to Samuel Richardson's best-seller, *Pamela*. Richardson's tale is ostensibly one of virtue rewarded; serving-maid Pamela repulses the repeated libidinous assaults of her employer Squire Booby, and eventually he marries her. Fielding saw the book as a coyly drawn-out, sensationalist description of panting lust and near-rape, in which a determined tease in the end gets greater worldly rewards by inflaming passions than by yielding to them.

At first Fielding wrote a short and rather clumsy pamphlet, *Shamela*, to expose what he saw as Richardson's hypocrisy. As a way of improving and extending his treatment he invented Pamela's brother, Joseph, and subjected him to the same assaults, this time by Squire B.'s wife Lady Booby, and her companion Mrs Slipslop. The big difference is that Joseph has no intention of being disloyal to his beloved Fanny back home. His reward for virtue is more realistic than his sister's: first he is dismissed, and then attacked and stripped by robbers. From this plight he is rescued by Parson Adams, Squire Booby's curate. Here the adventure proper begins, as the two good men try to make their way home through an hilariously wicked world.

The guileless virtue of Parson Adams is the novel's fulcrum. Succouring the distressed, discussing the beauties of Homer's poetry, and punching a publican on the nose, come equally naturally to the parson, and Fielding extracts much enjoyment for the reader from Adams's complete innocence of city ways, as evidenced by his mistaking a cure for venereal affliction as a form of spiritual retreat.

There is something strangely contemporary about some of Adams's encounters. Discussing charity with a rich fellow passenger who likes neither the word nor the idea, Adams says, 'Sir, my definition of charity is, a generous disposition to relieve the distressed,' to which the other replies, 'Alas! Mr Adams, who are meant by the distressed? Believe me, the distresses of mankind are mostly imaginary, and it would be rather folly than goodness to relieve them,' to which he adds that no one can be hungry in a country 'where excellent salads are to be gathered in every field', and as for nakedness: well, clothes are no more necessary for man than for beasts. Adams, finding that he prefers to walk, leaps from the carriage without asking it to stop.

Once encountered, Parson Adams and his refreshing view of the world – and his propensity for getting into trouble and falling into ditches, ponds and other declivities because he is 'lost in contemplation of a passage in Aeschylus', are unforgettable.

Richardson and Fielding between them invented the English novel. The latter has perhaps the greater claim than the former, who adapted the epistolary technique for fictional purposes whereas Fielding blended the example of Cervantes with realism, psychological perceptiveness and more complex structure. (The talent for burlesque of the third in the usual triumvirate, Smollett, has not weathered so well.) But it is Fielding's rich expression of an optimistic Enlightenment ethics that sets him apart, an outlook which, for all the comedy of its embodiment in Parson Adams, still offers one of the best hopes for civilising the world.

George Moore

How many forgotten masterpieces are there in the literature of the English tongue? More than one might think, I suspect. Without question one of them is George Moore's *Memoirs of My Dead Life* – neglected perhaps because of its unpropitious title, more likely because its contemporaries could not take its scandalous, irreverent, anarchic contents, its sharpness and unashamedness of wit, and what must have seemed its decadence; and therefore buried it beneath their opprobrium.

There is no other book in English like it. It resembles what one hears of the Comte de Maugny's accounts of courtesan opulence in the demi-monde of nineteenth-century Paris, except that it is hard to imagine such insouciance and flashing humour in any but a cosmopolitan of Moore's quicksilver stamp. He wrote in English of great beauty and refinement, a mordant, swift, sinuous prose marvellously apt for the impression he wished to give, which was of unstoppably good conversation. He was both an observer and a doer, a lover of women and pleasure, and at the same time a dedicated artist: his novels and autobiographical writings give rich testimony to how carefully he thought about the business of writing, and how marvellously – once his early realist period was over – he put that care into effect.

If Moore is remembered for anything now it is two novels, *Esther Waters* (made into a film with Dirk Bogarde in 1948) and *The Brook Kerith*. The first was published at the same time as Hardy's *Tess of the D'Urbervilles*, and with the same theme: a seduced girl. *The Brook Kerith* was published during the First World War and considers what would have happened to Jesus had he survived his nailing to the cross and taken himself into obscurity. One scene has Paul meet Jesus after proclaiming Jesus's death and resurrection, an encounter that serves to explain much about Moore's own rejection of religion.

Moore was the grandson of the President of the Republic of Ireland, an office that existed briefly during the French invasion of Ireland in 1798. He was the son of a wealthy Irish MP who committed suicide in 1873, leaving him, at the age of eighteen, very rich and wholly at leisure. He went to Paris, became a friend of Mallarmé and the Symbolists, met Manet, Dégas, Pissarro, Renoir and various Impressionists, got to know and admire Zola, and was among the first English writers to appreciate Verlaine, Rimbaud and Laforgue.

Critics of Moore are apt to say that his early work owed too much to his French sojourn, especially the documentary character, learned from Zola, of his early novels. And as if all his work is a matter of who influenced him, the critics continue by saying that it embodies the influence of this writer and that, principally Pater. The fact is that Moore was a careful student of his craft, with a lively interest in what his contemporaries were essaying; and he experimented throughout his long writing life with a sharp eye to form and execution. At his best he is one of the outstanding prose stylists of the language, and also one of the most protean and various of its authors.

But far from being derivative, he was himself a major influence on intellectual style in his time. He is a luminary of the Decadents in England, and whereas some think that Impressionism's reception in the Anglophone world had to wait for Roger Fry in 1912, Moore's *Modern Painters* of 1892 was the first to applaud them.

For a time after the Boer War, which disgusted Moore because of the jingoism in England and Kitchener's cruel concentration camps on the veld, he returned to Ireland and joined with Yeats and others in the Celtic revival movement. But nationalism and its associated pieties could not hold an intelligence like his for long, and he eventually returned to England where he lived until his death in 1933.

Moore published *Memoirs of my Dead Life* in 1906, and thereby outraged respectable opinion among his contemporaries. It is the first of three works of autobiography (the second itself three volumes long). Perhaps the *Memoirs* should not be classed as autobiography so much as reminiscence, and then almost exclusively of a sentimental or erotic kind. It is a recollection of loves and losses, of passions, of romantic journeys, of affairs and adulteries, all beautifully evoked and carefully, circumstantially, described – sometimes amusingly and sometimes tenderly. In telling of his amorous journey with Doris – she of the long curving fingers and milk-white legs – he describes looking forward to the moment when he can watch her undress: 'talking to her and watching her the while as she prepared herself for the night – looking on at the letting down of her hair and the brushing of it – a woman versed in the art of love prepares herself for bed so imperceptibly that any attempt to indicate a stage in her undressing breaks the harmony; for there is a harmony in the way she passes from the moment when she sits in her evening dress playing with her bracelets to the moment when she drops her night-gown over her head and draws her silk stockings off her legs, white as milk, kicking her little slippers aside before she slips over the edge and curls herself into the middle of a bed as broad as a battlefield.'

One of Moore's many quotable remarks is: 'A great artist is always before his time or behind it.' He was assuredly before his time. If anyone were to write a version of the *Memoirs* now it would scarcely seem revolutionary. But at the time of publication it was entirely original – a stream of recollection as a stream of consciousness, flowing without let or blush into all matters pertinently human (even a worry about whether he is going to be able to perform on the night of consummation: 'She was *une fille en marbre*, but not at all *une fille de marbre*; and, all preliminaries over, I went in unto her. Saved! Saved! by her beauty from the misfortune dreaded by all lovers'). It must have been breathtaking for contemporary readers to be plucked out of the peaceful business of opening a book, straight into a mesmerising account of deliciously remembered erotic adventure, for from the very first sentence Moore casts his spell and hurries the reader away, and he does not stop until the glorious notion in the last words of the last page: 'I believe that billions of years hence, billions and billions of years hence, I shall be sitting in the same room where I sit now, writing the same lines ... and that the same figures, the same nymphs, and the same fauns will dance around me again.'

Kuhn and Popper

Thomas Kuhn's slender volume *The Structure of Scientific Revolutions*, published in 1962, has become a modern classic in more domains of thought than just the philosophy of science. In total it has sold a million copies in twenty languages, and its central idea has become part of the wallpaper of thinking in many disciplines.

That central idea is as follows. Science undergoes periods of 'normal' activity in which generally accepted methods and aims define what count as appropriate areas of research and the right way to investigate them. But when difficulties accumulate, making the existing paradigm of enquiry unsustainable, a revolution occurs which introduces an entirely new paradigm that wholly replaces the old, constituting a new 'normal science' that operates until it, in its turn, is replaced by yet another 'paradigm shift', a phrase Kuhn made famous. Crucially, old and new paradigms are 'incommensurable'; the new is not an improvement on the old, it is just different, and the two cannot be compared.

Critics argue that this picture of science is harmful, because it supports the way that the dominant social institutions which control science and its funding confer legitimacy on their own preferred science and scientists, while excluding people and ideas different from or opposed to them. This was particularly dangerous in the Cold War context, according to one such critic, Steve Fuller, writing in his *Kuhn vs. Popper: The Struggle for the Soul of Science*, when only those prepared to conform to the establishment view were able to have scientific careers. If one thinks about the difference between the views of Kuhn and Karl Popper, another great name in twentieth-century philosophy of science, it is the latter's promotion of the critical spirit of scientific enquiry that in the view of critics like Fuller should be preferred.

Popper argued that science proceeds by 'conjecture and refutation'. Ideas, however generated, are submitted to rigorous testing in the form of efforts to prove them false. If they survive, they are not thereby guaranteed to be true, but they can be employed so long as they remain unrefuted. If they are 'falsified' by the test – and it is a mark of the scientific nature of a hypothesis that it specifies the conditions under which it is false – then it must be set aside, and a better hypothesis devised.

Although there are many problems with Popper's 'falsificationist' model, its ideal of rigorous empirical challenge is a healthy one, for it sees science as a rational and critical enquiry capable of progress. This is a picture more consistent with a democratic ideal of science free from the control of one or another kind of conservative establishment, whether political, social or scientific. Also applaudable is Popper's belief that non-scientists can legitimately criticise science for failing to abide by its own avowed standards. For these reasons critics like Fuller think that in the competition between the ideas of Kuhn and Popper, the wrong ideas – Kuhn's – won.

Kuhn and Popper only once participated in the same conference – in London in the summer of 1965 – but such was the disparity between their views that in the entire course of it they avoided direct engagement with one another. That often happens with contrasting visions, judging between which turns on evaluating their whole ethos, and the consequences that come from adopting it. But the key point surely lies in the fact that whereas Kuhn's model of scientific history is in effect non-teleological, in the sense that it cannot be described as getting us closer to the truth of things, Popper's retains contact with objectivity, at least as the aspiration of enquiry. For that reason Kuhn has been embraced by post-modernists and relativists, and Popper very much not. That difference is telling.

Mark Rothko's The Artist's Reality

For sixty years the manuscript of a book about art by no less a figure than Mark Rothko lay forgotten among his papers. His descendants had heard rumours about it, but until a secretary found it they were not certain of its existence.

They could not have guessed how fascinating and perhaps important the manuscript would prove to be. Rothko was an erudite, cultured, widely read and highly intelligent man who, as his book shows, had thought profoundly about the nature of art, especially painting, and who therefore had a systematic philosophy of art to offer.

Given that the book is incomplete, it would be rash to claim that it represents Rothko's final views. This is especially so given that the portrait Rothko here gives of art is not immediately recognisable as a portrait of his own art – a puzzle for the critics to resolve.

Such evidence as exists for determining when the book was written suggests the early 1940s. The date is significant because it marks a turning-point in Rothko's life. Until then his paintings had been figurative; afterwards they became abstract. During that period Rothko stopped painting, devoting himself instead to the study of philosophy and mythology. He also then suffered a nervous breakdown. No doubt haunted by war news and the fate of his native Russia, when he resumed painting it was to portray a strange disarray of human bodies and blasted landscapes.

The major output of that transitional period, it seems, was

this fascinating book. In it he defends and explains modern art – the art of the half-century preceding his writing of the book – by showing how it is a logical progression in art's unfolding history. His analysis of concepts that play a key role in his theory – plasticity, space and beauty – is illuminating and philosophically profound.

Art, Rothko says, is made because it fulfils a biological necessity for self-expression. It is a language which offers an effective means for satisfying this drive. That means that it is 'a species of nature', which 'like every other species, proceeds according to logic through stages of change that we can call growth'.

From a consideration of what is constant in this process of change, Rothko says, we can discern what a painting essentially is: namely, 'a statement of the artist's notions of reality in terms of plastic speech'. Painting is a form of generalisation, in the sense that it reduces everything to 'plastic elements' representing what can be grasped by the senses.

Rothko defines his crucial idea as follows: 'Plasticity is the presentation of a sense of movement in a painting.' The movement in question is that of recession and advancement of forms in space; just as figures in relief on the side of a silver bowl have to be tapped out to give the moulding required, so the handling of paint (sometimes literally, as in the case of those who use paint thickly in almost sculptural quantities) on the plane surface is intended to do its work either tactilely – as Berenson said Giotto did – or impressionistically, as Blashfield said Giotto failed to do (Giotto painted each individual blade of grass; but that is not how we see grass, Blashfield argued – we see a mass of green, and that therefore is how it should be painted).

The relationship between plasticity and space is fundamental. 'Space is the philosophical basis of a painting,' Rothko says; it is indeed 'the key to the meaning of the picture'. What modern art has done is to take to a logical conclusion the rapid development, from Giotto onwards, of the painter's under-standing and handling of space.

For Rothko the experience of beauty is 'the experience of rightness, reflected in an ideal of proportions, and as an apper-ception of harmoniousness, whose recognition produces an exaltation'. This remains true for what the critics of modern art see as distortion. But the 'distortions' of modern art, Rothko argues, are nothing more than logical developments of the dis-tortions practised by Dürer and Leonardo, and even more dra-matically by Signorelli, Michelangelo and the Venetians.

Whether or not one agrees with its arguments and insights, Rothko's book is fascinating as the testament of a major artist who had a deeply intellectual as well as practical understanding of what he did. As such it is required reading, and not just for students of Rothko's work. It is a tract central to the art of the twentieth century, not because it influenced anyone – it lay hidden too long; although it might now become an influence – but because it captures a moment of intense perception into the nature of art by one of its chief practitioners.

Rochester and the libertines

It is quite something to live in an age of riotous immorality, and yet to be accounted the most dissolute individual of the time. That is the achievement of the notorious John Wilmot, second Earl of Rochester, who lived very fast and died very young in the reign of Charles II. He is the subject of a film starring Johnny Depp as the handsome, witty, devastatingly charming and unstoppably immoral Earl. But however good the film is, and however many X-ratings it attracts, it can never capture all the truth about Rochester, for – surprising as it may seem – we live in a more prudish age than he did, and not all his doings can be reprised on the cinema screen.

Rochester was a poet of great talent, a brave naval officer, a rampantly intemperate bisexual, a 'harvester of maidenheads', a pimp and bawd for his King, a Hooray Henry repeatedly involved in duels and brawls (at least one of which resulted in the murder of a citizen of London) – and he died a victim, aged just thirty-three, of accumulated doses of both gonorrhoea and syphilis.

Charles II's reign is known as the Restoration because Charles was restored to the throne in 1660 after the republican Commonwealth period of Cromwell's rule. But it was the opposite of a restoration in moral terms. In England under Cromwell an austere and pleasure-denying form of Puritan Christianity set the dominant standard of behaviour. The Restoration brought to England a royal court that had taught itself very different manners and morals during its exile in France. The effect on the aristocracy, which had chafed under the restraint of Cromwell's years, was electrifying. Back on top socially and politically, enjoying revenues of estates distrained from the regicides who had toppled Charles I, and given the licence of Charles II's own example as an energetic womaniser and reveller, the leading members of Charles's court let themselves go – and with a vengeance.

If proof were needed of the power of the arts to influence public sentiment and behaviour, Restoration theatre with its witty, bawdy plays, and the magnificent portraits in oils of the King's mistresses – among them the actress Nell Gwyn, the nymphomaniacal Lady Castlemaine, and Louise de Keroualle, Duchess of Portsmouth – would surely provide it. Rochester added a further dimension with the explicit obscenity of his poetry and his own excursions into playwriting, most notably his *Sodom*. One of his best-known poems, 'A Ramble in St James's Park', begins, 'Much wine had passed with grave discourse/Of who fucks who and who does worse'; in his 'Song of a Young Lady to her Ancient Lover' he has the Young Lady say, 'Thy nobler part, which but to name/In our sex would be counted shame,/By Age's frozen grasp possessed,/From his ice shall be released,/And soothed by my reviving hand,/In former warmth and vigour stand.'

In *Sodom* Rochester satirises the court of Charles II under stinging pseudonyms: the King himself appears as Bolloximian; his wife, Queen Catherine, as Cuntagratia; Lady Castlemaine as Fuckadilla, the King's brother (and later James II) as Buggeranthus; Louise de Keroualle as Clytoris; and Louis XIV of France as Tarsehole the King of Gomorrah. Some of Rochester's contemporaries were outraged by his free use of language; his defenders claimed that since obscenities are 'too gross to inflame desire', Rochester's real purpose was to restrain venal appetites by disgusting them before they could have ill effect. This implausible suggestion has the stamp of Rochester's own cheerful wit about it.

A well-known indication of the times is provided by Samuel Pepys's diary, in which the assiduous civil servant's perpetual peccadilloes with mistresses and prostitutes are faithfully recorded. Yet in comparison to the hell-raising aristocrats among whom Rochester moved, Pepys was a model of virtue. When Rochester returned from his Grand Tour as a very young man, the circle of dissolutes he joined had as its nucleus the Duke of Buckingham, Lord Buckhurst, Sir Charles Sedley and Sir Henry Savile, all already experienced rakes, and nine-tenths along the road to perdition. He quickly outpaced them all.

They were all members of the Ballers' Club, dedicated to drink and debauchery. Sex was a principal feature of the members' activities. Sexual exhibitions and demonstrations, orgies and naked dancing with the girls at 'Lady' Bennett's brothel, the club's headquarters, figured among other delights. But none of the Ballers had Rochester's skill as a deflowerer of virgins, because none of them had his looks and charm. He was soon famous for the ease with which he got girls into bed. Part of his motive for doing so was to provide the King with fresh pleasures, for he not only deflowered virgins but thereafter taught them tricks and amorous arts which he knew, as a Lord of the Bedchamber who had often conducted the King's mistresses and whores to the royal bed, would be to Charles's taste.

Charles II was a consistently good patron to Rochester, despite being offered severe provocation at times to be otherwise. Part of the reason was that Rochester's father, the first Earl, had been a staunch champion of Charles II's cause during the Cromwellian period, and had fought bravely for the royal cause in both military and political ways. He died before Charles became King. Charles therefore had a debt of gratitude to his son. Secondly, Rochester's delightfully witty conversation made him a jewel in company, and he was much loved by the court.

Thirdly, his usefulness as a procurer of sexual pleasures for the King was a service Charles did not want to lose.

So even when Rochester fell foul of the law, Charles intervened to save him. And Rochester certainly needed saving. He tried to abduct an heiress (this earned him several days in the Tower of London, and he later married the lady and her great dowry); he fought several duels (highly illegal); boxed someone's ears in the King's presence (an act technically counting as treason, which earned Rochester a brief exile in France); and was somehow involved in the death of a watchman who had tried to arrest him among a rowdy gang of drunk aristocrats.

After a while, though, Rochester began to test the King's patience with his lampoons and satires. One of them so enraged Charles that he banished Rochester from his presence for several weeks – though, as before, Rochester was soon back in favour. But the incident did not teach Rochester a lesson; he continued his increasingly unacceptable acts of lèse-majesté, with the inevitable consequence of a breach at last. His poetic comparisons between Charles's penis and his sceptre might be forgivable – perhaps, indeed, flattering – but the little poem that finally turned the King against Rochester was the now well-known 'God bless our good and gracious King/Whose promise none relies on/Who never said a foolish thing/Nor ever did a wise one.'

Charles claimed that when he was drinking and debauching with his favourite courtiers, they could say what they liked and he would not take offence; but the truth was that he did take offence, and this little verse proved a poison pellet. Shortly afterwards Rochester gave the King an excuse to withdraw his patronage: following a drunken revel, Rochester smashed a beautiful and priceless sundial in Charles's privy garden. He was never again to bask in the King's approval.

The immorality or at least amorality of the Restoration has led to it being called a 'libertine' period. Charles and his courtiers had acquired the habit of thinking and acting as they pleased while in exile in France, by which time 'thinking and acting as one pleased' had become the kind of hedonistic excess exemplified by Rochester. But libertinism had not started that way; indeed, it had not started as a form of sexual and alcoholic licence at all.

The word 'libertine' was first applied in the 1550s to a sect of Protestants in northern Europe who, with unimpeachable logic, reasoned that since God had ordained all things, nothing could be sinful. They proceeded to act accordingly. Their views were regarded with horror by both Catholics on one side and Calvinists on the other, for whom the word 'libertine' therefore came to mean depravity and debauchery in the highest degree. This is now the standard meaning of the term. By association it also came to apply to anyone suspected of rejecting religion. In the early decades of the seventeenth century that was indeed the word's main meaning, and it was taken to denote anyone with an interest in science and philosophy.

The reason for the seventeenth-century application of the term 'libertine' to people with intellectual interests (whether or not they were also atheists – which was far from invariably so; many of those with scientific interests were believers) was that orthodox Christians assumed that advanced thinking must lead to dissolute morals. This non sequitur was so fixed in the public mind by the late seventeenth century that in order to maintain a distinction between immoralists and people of a scientific bent, the word 'libertine' was reserved to the former and the latter came to be called 'free thinkers' or 'philosophes' instead.

In the reigns of Charles II in England and Louis XIV in France, morals and language were equally free (moralisers would say: coarse and degraded), so that those who were libertines in the intellectual sense were also quite likely to keep several mistresses, visit brothels and lard their talk with profanities and oaths, all of which was perfectly acceptable to everyone other than the prim among their contemporaries. It is no accident that the Duke of Buckingham had a handsomely appointed chemistry laboratory in his house, and Rochester himself was a student both of chemistry and medicine in the intervals between seducing women and boys.

There would almost certainly have been no libertinism, and therefore no Rochester, without what some historians call the 'libertine crisis' in France in the 1620s. This was a significant episode for many reasons, one of which is that it marked a crucial moment in the birth of the modern world. Of course this parturition took much bloody and painful struggle over a much longer period, starting with Luther and the theses he nailed to the church door in Wittenberg in 1517. But the 1620s have a special significance because it was the decade that saw the last gasp of reactionary religion's efforts to stop the new world of science and philosophy coming into being.

In fact the 'libertine crisis' began in 1619 at Toulouse, when an itinerant teacher of philosophy and medicine called Giulio Cesare Vanini was burned at the stake. His crime was 'atheism' (but also, by implication, homosexuality). His name became a byword throughout Europe for atheism and the 'naturalism' that accompanied it – that is, the view that nature is the ultimate reality and source of all things.

Vanini started as a monk, studying theology and medicine in Italy before travelling throughout Europe, working as a tutor or secretary in noble households. He got into trouble for homosexuality and for killing a man in a brawl, and therefore escaped to England for a time, where he abjured his Catholicism. On returning to France he earned his keep by giving private lessons. In Toulouse, an ardently orthodox city, one of his pupils denounced him for teaching that men had no souls but died as other animals did, and that the Virgin Mary was an ordinary woman who needed to have sex in order to get pregnant. The city authorities decided that he was attracting too many youths to his lectures, so to get rid of him they put him on trial and condemned him to death. While being led to the stake Vanini cried out in his native Italian, 'I die cheerfully as befits a philosopher!'

The Europe-wide chorus of vilification that rose around Vanini's name took its cue from a violently hostile pamphlet written by a Jesuit called François Garasse. As a result of the Vanini affair a mood set in which expressed the fear of the old world at what the dawning new world was doing to established certainties. Vanini's execution was followed by a number of other high-profile attacks on 'libertine' thinkers. One was the execution in Paris in 1622 of Jean Fontanier, an occultist who taught mystic doctrines he had allegedly learned while travelling in the East. In 1623 the poet Theophile de Viau was arrested on suspicion of atheism, and was tortured, tried and condemned to death; but in 1625 his sentence was commuted to banishment, almost certainly because he was well-connected among the French aristocracy, and admired by Paris's cognoscenti.

There is much in common between de Viau and Rochester; the former is practically a French prototype of the latter. The fact that the proximate cause of de Viau's trial was his 'obscene' poetry and suspicions of homosexuality might appear to suggest that charges of atheism were polite masks for attacks on obscenity and homosexuality. In reality, the latter were taken to be expressive of atheism, or identical with it. For how – so the reasoning went – could anyone soil his hands with either if he were a person of true Christian faith? Rochester was likewise believed to be an atheist, and much was made of the fact that when he lay dying in agony from the effects of venereal disease he supposedly 're-converted' to Anglicanism.

But whereas the libertines of the 1620s in France risked arrest and execution for the impieties implied by their erotic poems and sexual practices, in England a mere generation later not only were such things no longer criminal, but actually the norm at the King's court. How things had changed! The freedom of thought that had been won by the rejection of the old world of religious orthodoxy had spread itself into freedom of action – a process that tight-lipped folk will deprecate, pointing at Rochester's fate as due punishment; the rest of us might give thanks that the scientific revolution which opened minds and hearts also led to the antibiotics which, had they existed in Rochester's day, would have saved him.

There has been no other period in British history in which morals were quite as they were in Rochester's time. To a large extent the sexual freedom enjoyed today is comparable, and the acceptance of homosexuality is greater; while the louche lifestyle of this celebrity model or that pop-star seem positively Rochester-like.

But the licence accorded those with position and wealth in Restoration society gave them a degree of latitude, and an immunity from consequences, which would now (if discovered) not be tolerated. This means that the aristocratic roués and rakehells of Restoration England could do almost anything they wanted and get away with it, very often under the protection of the King himself, and that is why their excesses were so great. In this one respect things are now much better than they then were.

I doubt, though, whether they are better in all other respects, for a lot of what history has called debauch is really just fun. Rochester, at least, certainly managed to have his share of it.

Laurence Sterne

There is nothing like Laurence Sterne's immortal *Life and Opinions of Tristram Shandy* elsewhere in the literature of the English language. Without form or plot, a stew of unforgettable characters and hilarious incidents, it makes art out of wit, bawdy and sentiment – and yet it seems to have sprung from nowhere into the mind of a middle-aged, disappointed, unhappily-married clergyman in Yorkshire who had published no fiction beforehand, and given no previous indication of wanting to.

The publication of *Tristram Shandy* made Sterne instantly famous. This was the result of not only the book's merits – and notoriety: for many who found its comedy irresistible were also scandalised by the fact that its author was a parson – but of Sterne's energetic and astute promotion of the first two volumes. He claimed to have written *Tristram Shandy* 'not to be fed but to be famous', which is not quite true; tired of waiting for preferment in the corrupt embrace of the eighteenth-century Church, and subsisting on modest means despite being a pluralist (with two parish livings and a York Minster prebend), Sterne had decided to take his fate into his own hands.

The result was spectacular. Very soon after *Tristram Shandy* first appeared in late 1759 Sterne became the toast of London, and was lionised by its highest society. He revelled in invitations from lords, bishops and royalty, and in the first instance made money by the bucketful. After the heady delights of London life he found it hard to bear the isolation of the Yorkshire parsonage where his quarrelsome wife lived. And by that time – Sterne was forty-six when *Tristram Shandy* was published – he was already beginning to decline in health, increasingly troubled by tuberculosis, and perhaps also afflicted by the onset of tertiary syphilis. Either way he had only eight more years to live. He left his parishes in the care of curates, and began the first of two long sojourns on the continent of Europe, marvellously recorded in the closing volumes of *Tristram* and in his other great work, *A Sentimental Journey*.

When Sterne first arrived in Paris he found that his reputation had preceded him, and he was as celebrated there as he had been in London. He dined with Baron d'Holbach, whose salon was at the centre of intellectual life in the French Enlightenment; and on his return visit he sparred over a dinner table with no less a person than the great David Hume, philosopher, historian and luminary of the British Enlightenment. To see an author leap from the obscurity of a country parsonage to the first circles of intellect and society in so short a space is a tribute to the power of literature, and there is something positively Shandean about some aspects of it – especially the fact that most of England's bishops loved *Tristram Shandy*, but felt obliged to asperse its morals.

The salient fact about *Tristram Shandy* is that Tristram himself scarcely figures in the book, apart from such brief manifestations as the unlucky circumstances of his conception, which hilariously commences the epic. The real hero of the book is Uncle Toby, and the book is a picaresque adventure of his thoughts, sensations, conversations and eccentricities, along with those of the rest of the vivid supporting cast. It is hard to anticipate who will find the book funny, but it is a work capable of reducing the gloomiest soul to helpless laughter, by a mixture of absurdity and moral slapstick, and the sheer craziness of the perspective from which everything in Shandyland seems as if skewed out of true.

There is a remarkable codicil to the tale of Sterne's life. His daughter Lydia, the only one of his children to survive infancy, showed as astute a commercial publishing sense as he himself had. When he died leaving her and her mother almost destitute (for though he had found late that he knew how to make money, he knew better how to spend it), Lydia immediately collected his unpublished sermons and letters, and brought out editions of them. There is something modern and endearing about this businesslike style of grief; and Sterne, who loved her, would have approved – as would Uncle Toby, and Tristram himself.

Lawrence Durrell

L awrence Durrell was an exile. Born in India to a long-standing colonial family of the functionary class, then briefly educated in England at a minor public school in fulfilment of his father's aspirations to social advancement, he was never able to accept England (which he called 'Pudding Island') and its attitudes, and therefore chose to make his exile permanent. He lived in Greece, Egypt, briefly in Argentina, and for many years in France; anxious to sink roots, he devoted intense study to the places he occupied, wrote about them marvellously in his travel books, and used them as the theatre of his fiction and poetry. He had the exile's vivid sense of place, and of how people are shaped by it. For himself, although he loved Greece and Provence, he felt that his home was a country he had never visited, but had seen from his boyhood home in Darjeeling, floating not just above the earth but, it seemed, in the heavens themselves. This distantly viewed, unknown country was Tibet, the tragic holy land now raped and imprisoned by its Chinese invaders.

There is no natural slot in twentieth-century English literature for Durrell's creative work. He was an experimental novelist, a cerebral sensualist, brilliantly – even exorbitantly – gifted with words; and yet both his poetry and his novels somehow fall short. The reason is a paradoxical one: he devoted much energy to the elaborate construction of his fiction, and his poems often display subtle underlying order. But he was unable to discipline fully the luxuriousness of his verbal powers.

Words gushed out of him like a fountain of sparkling wine, and they made him heady; he could not cut, weed, or chasten them enough. The result is a diminution of art. His letters and his travelogues show what he could be: the letters in their sheer pyrotechnic virtuosity of language make one gasp with pleasure, and the travel writings are luminous under their externally imposed form. But the obscurity and trickery of the poems, and the expressive disorganisation of most of the fiction, are serious faults. Nevertheless, the *Alexandria Quartet* in particular deserves a place in the history of English literature for more than its liberating ideas and innovative methods, for it is the production of a great writerly imagination.

Although Durrell acquired much from the time he spent living with Henry Miller and Anaïs Nin in pre-war Paris, the man who most consistently tried to make him think about his writing was his editor at Faber, T. S. Eliot. At one point Eliot asked him whether he was a poet or a novelist, and challenged him to choose. At the end of his life Durrell told interviewers that he was a poet, but that some of his poetry took the form of prose fiction. That seems right; what is also right was Durrell's refusal to accept Eliot's sharp insistence on separating the two and choosing just one.

In the quarrel between Proust and Sainte-Beuve, the latter argued that we need biographies of writers to understand their work, whereas the former thought that the work comes from somewhere no biographer, and not even the subject himself or herself, can understand. Both are right, but for different kinds of writers. Durrell's work benefits from his biographers, and he has been fortunate to have good ones, chief among them Gordon Bowker and Ian MacNiven. The former provides a sympathetic and often highly perceptive account of Durrell in which the darker side of his imagination – his interest in sex, sadism, incest, the occult and astrology – are brought into informative connection with his work.

Biographers can reasonably aspire to understand their subjects better than they understood themselves, if only because they see the completed picture in the perspective offered by time. Durrell's biographers succeed in this way; they show us why, despite those sides of his character which are unappealing at least – his frequently disgusting treatment of his wives, his inexpungeable schoolboyish egocentricity – he is nevertheless an intensely interesting figure.

In conformity with modern fashion, Durrell's death in late 1990 was shortly followed by charges that he had committed incest with his daughter Sappho, who had committed suicide a few years before, and who had left a journal detailing her unhappy struggles with mental instability and broken relationships. The evidence in the case is examined by the biographers, who conclude that Sappho Durrell's own description of the matter as 'psychological incest' is probably most accurate. After the death of his most loved wife, Claude, Durrell leaned on Sappho; later he had affairs with women her age or younger, and Sappho saw a cruel significance in the fact. The controversy merely reinforces the modern truth that allegations of sin are the wages of celebrity.

It also raises a point left aside in the Proust–Sainte-Beuve difference of view. Should biography not just seek to illuminate a life, and perhaps judge its contribution, but also make a moral assessment? And if the latter, supposing it to be negative, should that be a reason for diminishing the value of the work? I think and hope that this should be so in very few cases – in the egregious ones only, where the work itself is the immoral thing, as with Adolf Hitler or Otto Weininger. For the rest, the difficult grain of human nature and experience, once death has rubbed it smooth, deserves not condemnation but sympathy.

Russell on happiness

In the early part of his long career, in fact until the mid-1920s, Bertrand Russell believed that philosophy was strictly a technical subject – in fact, a branch of logic – which had nothing to do with matters of ordinary life. He still held this view during the time that he lived and taught in Peking in the early 1920s, which meant that he lost an opportunity to help the young Chinese intellectuals who asked him for guidance in matters social and political, which they much needed at that tumultuous period of China's history. The American Pragmatist philosopher John Dewey was also in China at that time, and did not hesitate to respond to such requests, with the result that he is remembered today in China with some reverence, whereas Russell left scarcely any mark outside Peking University.

But Russell's austere technical view of philosophy did not last much longer. His reputation as a philosopher prompted people to ask him for his opinion about every imaginable subject, and when he found it convenient to write non-technical books and articles as a way of making money, he found a readership eager to know what a philosopher could say on the pressing questions of life and morality which, afresh in every generation, interest the more reflective members of the public. Such people could of course go to the writings of the great thinkers of the past, among them the philosophers of classical antiquity, to help them work things out for themselves; and some do. But a special interest always attaches to what philosophers of one's own day think, because they share the very same experience and problems as oneself, which gives their perspective an added value. It was this need that Russell found himself able to meet when at last he turned his attention to it.

The seeds of the change in Russell's attitude to 'popular philosophy' had in fact been sown during the First World War. He had campaigned throughout that horrendous event as an anti-war activist, twice falling foul of the law as a result, and having to spend some months in prison. He wrote and lectured much in relation to his campaign, but at that time did not think of the work as an aspect of the philosophical enterprise. The idea that a thinker might be engaged with the pressing questions of the day, trying to bring to bear considerations of principle and the resources of thought from the great moral and political debates of the history of philosophy, for some strange reason seemed alien to British philosophers in the last decades of the nineteenth century and the first six decades of the twentieth century, during which academic teachers of philosophy expressly disavowed any interest in or responsibility for them. What makes this surprising is that Russell's own (secular) god-father, John Stuart Mill, was anything but a disengaged philo-sopher, but rather a shining example of one who – as with his father John Mill and his father's mentor Jeremy Bentham – tries to do his bit to improve the world.

By the mid and late 1920s, Russell had made the connection between the sort of work he had done when campaigning against the First World War, and the constant invitations he was receiv-ing to address the needs of contemporary society. Moreover, he thought that education was the key to preventing wars and benefiting the future, as did many other intellectuals at the time (among them Karl Popper and Ludwig Wittgenstein, who also chose to become teachers), and therefore he decided to open a school. All these factors led to his rejoining the great tradition of philosophers who have been teachers and guides as well as scholars, and the result was the beginning of many years of writing, lecturing and campaigning on a wide range of matters, from education and morals to the threat of nuclear weapons.

To see how fully Russell's change into a public philosopher possessed him, one need only look at the following small sample from his enormous list of writings: *On Education, Especially in Early Childhood* (1926), published that same year in America as *Education and the Good Life* and later abridged as *Education of Character*. In 1927 he published *Why I am not a Christian*, in 1929 *Marriage and Morals*, and in 1930 *The Conquest of Happiness*. All this time he was writing articles on these and related themes, among them a weekly 600-word column for the Hearst newspapers in America, in which he dispensed elegantly-tailored snippets of observation and wisdom, some of them little gems. Both *Why I am not a Christian* and *Marriage and Morals* proved enduringly controversial. The latter lost Russell his appointment at the City College of New York in 1940 on the grounds of its immorality, and ten years later won him the Nobel Prize for Literature.

The most distinctive thing about Russell's views in these non-technical, social and moral spheres is their resolute common sense, lucidity and open-mindedness. Think of the contrast between, say, a French savant waving his Gauloise about and lucubrating profoundly, in obscure language, about life, sex and ideas, and then look at the clarity, openness and good will of Russell's writings on the same subjects. Among too many of the intellectual brotherhood, clarity and openness is scorned as being too simple, even simplistic, the argument being that it perforce ignores all nuance, all subtlety, all profundity. This is a spurious objection. Some of the deepest truths are simple, when seen in the clearest light, and it takes a lucid intellect to grasp them so thoroughly that their simplicity can be brought into that light and offered to all, not just the privileged few. There is a perennial suspicion that Gauloise-waving intellectuals deliberately obfuscate to exclude *hoi polloi* and to retain their mystique as thinkers, and this, alas, is too often true, as anyone can determine for themselves by making the effort to transform the pundit's profundities into plain language, thus seeing what they really have to offer. One finds that they do not often offer the unaffected good sense supplied by Russell in his luminous, witty and pellucid prose.

Because Russell speaks so eloquently for himself, it is unnecessary to provide an interpretation here of what he says in *The Conquest of Happiness*. To get an overview of the book, simply look at the chapter headings. They convey Russell's fundamental message – for which he claims no originality, of course, but every support from the experience of mankind – that happiness is gained by being outward-looking in work and relationships, instead of wrapped up in oneself, dwelling on anxieties and fears. Look at the reasons, the examples, the insights he offers in considering these simple, apparently obvious but powerfully true thoughts, and remember that Russell had learned them from bitter personal experience. His former pupil Ludwig Wittgenstein once said that the proper task of philosophy is to remind ourselves of what we already know to be true; this is what Russell does here.

I might mention a respect in which that plain-speaking and unpretentious guide to happiness first affected my own life. I read this book as a teenager, and since then have occasionally thumbed through it partly to enjoy Russell's prose for its own sake, and partly to be reminded that plain and sensible truths can be well and memorably expressed. One of the ideas that stuck in my mind and invariably helped when its help was required, was the advice to ask oneself, when tossing about in trouble, whether one can do anything at that moment to deal with the problem. If yes, then do it; if no, then set the matter aside until one can. Lying awake thinking about an overdraft at two o'clock in the morning is a good example of where such advice proves its usefulness: for – *mirabile dictu* – applying it really works, and it has the wonderful ancillary effect of putting problems into their right perspective.

There will always be cynics to say that we need no ghost from the grave to tell us that happiness is the result of active outward engagement with life and the world. But since this is a truth, and one that makes a great difference to anyone who will accept and apply it, I think it is worth attending to – especially in Russell's elegant, witty and educative statement of it, which adds to its force, and thereby helps us remember it in the face of all pressures to do otherwise.

Voltaire's *Candide*, or optimism

Anyone asked to describe Voltaire's miniature masterpiece *Candide* would say that it is a satire on optimism, and they would be right – but for the wrong reasons. Yes, *Candide* wittily, entertainingly, even sometimes bleakly satirises optimism, which gave Voltaire a chance to attack many of mankind's follies in the process. But does that mean he was a pessimist, convinced that the cause of humanity is hopeless? No; and understanding why not is the same as seeing why most people would be right for the wrong reasons about *Candide*.

There are four 'isms' at issue in *Candide:* optimism, meliorism, quietism and pessimism. In eighteenth-century terms, optimism is the view that the world is the best world there can be, which is guaranteed by the fact that it was created by God, and God is both all-good and all-powerful. Meliorism is the view that the world is not perfect – is indeed very far from being so – but it can be made better; 'ameliorated' literally means 'sweetened'. Pessimism means that almost everything, if not indeed everything, is bad, and will never get better.

Quietism belongs to this family of 'isms' in an indirect way. It means accepting things as they are, keeping out of the line of fire, and getting on with life quietly. It therefore combines a bit of pessimism with a relieving garnish of meliorism.

In *Candide* Dr Pangloss is the high representative of optimism. Actually, he is a high caricature of optimism, for Voltaire deliberately – for artistic and polemical reasons – distorts the views of Dr Pangloss's hero, the philosopher Leibniz, in a rather interesting way. More on this in a moment. The melancholy Martin is *Candide*'s pessimist, and he has an easy time stating his case, because whereas all the accidents and misfortunes which occur to Pangloss and Candide are repeated refutations of Panglossian optimism, nothing – not even episodes of great good fortune – can refute Martin, for he need only gloomily say, 'Wait and see; this could all go wrong.'

Candide himself finishes by being a quietist. When the group of friends end their tumultuous adventures in Constantinople, and acquire a little garden there, Candide is the one who encourages them to tend it in quietness, no longer fretting over questions (still less endeavours) concerning the best and the worst of things.

And Voltaire himself is the meliorist in *Candide*, where a kind of success, a kind of happiness, a kind of 'best', is at last wrested from the grip of a multiply contrary fate for all the parties. And not only there but in his overall philosophy in life and work beyond *Candide* he is a meliorist. Had he not been so, he would not have written so much, and argued so long, in hopes of making the world a better place.

This is the respect in which Voltaire is a true Enlightenment figure, despite having savaged optimism so thoroughly in *Candide*. The Enlightenment is above all a meliorist project, and in *Candide* Voltaire singles out many of the things – superstition, greed, disloyalty, ignorance, selfishness, illiberalism – which conspire to make the world a bad place. For note one shining fact about *Candide*. The principal characters in it are all good people: the cheerful, hopeful Dr Pangloss; the delightful, ingenuous Candide; the excellent, faithful Cacambo; the honest Martin; the charming ever-innocent Paquette; even the much victimised and abused Cunegunde – all are examples of what would gladden a meliorist's heart, and even the heart of an optimist, in the proper sense of this term, which must now be explained.

For the philosopher Gottfried Wilhelm Leibniz, the conclusion that our world is the best of all possible worlds follows,
as already mentioned, from the perfections of God's nature.
It follows indeed with logical necessity, for it would not be
consistent with the beneficence and omnipotence of the deity
that he should create anything less than the best possible world.
But the best possible world need not be, and perhaps had better
not be, a *perfect* world. On the contrary, said Leibniz, the *best
possible* world might well be one in which the creatures it
contains are subjected to the test of miseries and struggles –
earthquake, plague, bereavement, injustice, struggle and the
like – in the interests of whatever ultimate plan the deity has
for them. A *perfect* world would contain nothing that would
test or stretch God's creatures; so a perfect world would not
necessarily be the best one for the deity's purposes, and therefore
our own ultimate good. By this logic Leibniz was able to make
the existence of an all-good and all-powerful God consistent
with the fact of the world's profound imperfections and the
moral and natural evils that everywhere infect it.

Voltaire did not like this casuistical way out of a problem that
challenged the faith of all reflective people. Europe had seen the
terrifying earthquake and tsunami that devastated Lisbon in
1755, an event that gave added force to the rejection of traditional religion shared by most of the Age of Reason's greatest
thinkers, he among them. That was his reason for caricaturing
optimism by misinterpreting the phrase 'best of all possible
worlds' as 'perfect world'. This is why Dr Pangloss, for all that
he was a votary of the rigorously logical Leibniz, used an array
of such illogical arguments as that we have noses so that we
can wear spectacles, putatively thereby proving that in this best
of all possible worlds, everything is for the best.

In any case, a book that was genuinely pessimistic could not
have El Dorado in it. Voltaire's version of Utopia – a place
without religious strife and without greed, a place of amity

between people because there is no cause for them to betray, cheat, fight and murder each other – is a place in fact of melioration. Candide manages to recreate, imperfectly of course, a miniature El Dorado at the end of the saga, showing where Voltaire's own best hopes lay.

In the summer of 1739 Voltaire and his extraordinary and brilliant mistress, Emilie du Châtelet, made a brief sojourn in Brussels. While there Voltaire styled himself 'the Ambassador of Utopia' on his invitation cards, and found to his amusement that hardly anyone got the joke – they did not know what 'utopia' meant or where it was. Yet in light of Voltaire's lifelong utopian quest for freedom – of thought, of conscience, of expression, of love, of the individual, of nations, of mankind at large – the title he adopted in jest surely applies to him in earnest.

France in Voltaire's day was an ugly and severely illiberal police state pullulating with what police states invariably produce: informers, schemers, libellers, sneaks, cheats, backstabbers and the like. Voltaire's outlook, as the herald of Enlightenment not just in France but the eighteenth-century world in general, meant that he had to fight on a number of fronts simultaneously: the Church, the state apparatus of censorship (whose punishments could be very severe), the sneaks and backstabbers who could make a profit out of getting him into trouble whether by real or imaginary means, and his own not always governable temperament.

Even while he was with the wonderful Emilie du Châtelet – gifted mathematician, scientist, authoress and translator into French of Newton – in their idyll at her château at Cirey, he was not safe from his enemies or himself, despite the fact that she attempted to restrain him, and kept his more inflammatory writings under lock and key to protect him from the consequences of their getting into the hands of the thought police in Paris.

But Voltaire was incorrigible. Early in his career he experienced both the Bastille and exile, profiting from the latter by getting to know and admire England and the Netherlands as places that flourished because of their liberty and religious tolerance. The beliefs and principles he acquired early he did not relinquish, even as they continued to get him into trouble. But, as Roger Pearson shows in *Voltaire Almighty: A Life in Pursuit of Freedom*, they also gave him many opportunities to keep his optimism alive. For a while it seemed that Frederick of Prussia might prove to be a monarch after Enlightenment hearts (the hope did not last very long), and in some of his closest relationships he had the pleasure of being with like-minded others, who not only appreciated his genius – all his contemporary world did as much – but gave him the relief of being able to express it in private.

Interested parties should read *Voltaire Almighty*, which will come as a revelation, especially if what they associate with the name of Voltaire is chiefly *Candide* and the *Philosophical Dictionary*. For Voltaire's first reputation was as a dramatist, with a number of theatrical hits to his name, and as a poet, whose 'Henriade' was the cornerstone of his early fame. But he was also a scientist (he had a laboratory at the château in Cirey, where among other experimental endeavours he attempted to weigh fire) and a philosopher. Many witty folk are such that their talents in conversation and social intercourse die with them; Voltaire's satirical humour survives because apart from his writings he burned such bright memories on the minds of those who knew him, whether friends or enemies.

Polemical engagement in the great question of God and man absorbed considerable amounts of Voltaire's energy as he grew to a famous old age in his retreat at Ferney near the Swiss border. He constituted himself 'the high priest of Deism', in Pearson's phrase, and among many other things wrote responses to the views of Baron d'Holbach and Spinoza. But the question of God was far from the only one. Satire and verse poured from him, and short alphabetically listed essays forming what amounted to his own version of the *Encyclopédie* – and all this in the midst of continuing to write drama, engaging in polemic, and living as simultaneously the most famous and notorious man of his age right into his eighties.

His death matched his life. He pushed away the priest who had arrived at his death-bed to ask whether he 'recognised the divinity of Jesus Christ', turned his back, and said, 'Let me die in peace.' His last thought was for the woman who had been the companion of his last twenty years, Marie-Louise Denis, in fact his niece but much more than a nurse and chatelaine. He died rich, but of course not just in money terms, because he left a treasury of works to posterity, and an abiding legacy as an iconic individual.

Vermeer's 'Girl interrupted'

A mong many reasons for appreciating Vermeer's works is their educative power. Anyone seeking to know how to read paintings can learn much from him. His pictures school one's sensibility rather as playing a B-major scale on the piano helps form correct hand position; just as that scale moulds the hands naturally into proper pianistic shape, so contemplation of a Vermeer naturally prompts a viewer to see his multiple and related intentions in composition, symbol, narrative and mood, and how he achieves their effect through the poetry of light.

'Girl interrupted at her music' is compositionally one of the simplest of Vermeer's works (another reason, perhaps, for the slight insecurity of attribution of this damaged and overpainted work; but it looks very much a Vermeer even to amateur eyes). A young girl sits at a table under a window – that Vermeer table, that Vermeer window, this time with elaborate mullioning – holding sheets of music in her hands. Her music tutor stands behind her, the spread of his arms and the volume of his cloak framing her. She is looking directly at the viewer, called from her study of the score as if by someone speaking, or something happening, in the viewer's vicinity. On the wall behind the figures is a painting of Cupid with left arm raised, as if about to cast his dart, or perhaps in a gesture of triumph at having made someone fall in love.

Internal connections among Vermeer's works immediately invite comparisons. The same girl, a little older, appears in 'Officer with a laughing girl'. This time she is dressed for visitors; in 'Interrupted' she is in everyday homely wear. The theme of music is characteristic in Vermeer, where it exploits the symbolic link between music and amorous possibilities. 'Young woman standing at a virginal' has the same Cupid painting on the back wall, and again the girl looks directly at the viewer, as if with a challenge; though in 'A lady writing a letter', the girl – beautifully dressed in the spotted-fur-lined golden robe that is a feature of several Vermeer canvases – gives a direct look at the viewer that conveys thoughtfulness instead.

Music and Cupid suggest a tale of amour in 'Interrupted', but as usual it has the teasing ambiguity of all Vermeer's narratives, which he skilfully relates by his choice of which moment in the story to portray. Is the tutor unrequitedly in love with the pupil? Do they feel the stirrings of mutual passion? The beauty of the painting lies in the delicate quotations of light on the finials of the heavy upright dining-room chairs, and in its full blossom on the exquisite curve of the lute's sound-box and the shining white sheets of music paper.

But psychological mystery is equally part of the beauty in Vermeer's work, and here the unsurprised, incurious look of the girl's direct gaze at the viewer suggests that her real attention is elsewhere – perhaps still with what the tutor is indicating on the page they hold together, more interestingly still if it is a love ballad they are sharing, whose lyrics constitute a message to her.

The closest relation to this painting elsewhere in Vermeer is 'The glass of wine'. Here the figures are dressed in visiting clothes, the same mullioned window has stained glass as if dressed for a visit too, and a different painting hangs on the rear wall. But the same wine carafe has come meaningfully into play, the same lute and music are now set well aside, suggesting – if one put the paintings into significant relationship – that everything has developed, and the girl is accepting from the man something that will change her outlook.

One might think of Vermeer's paintings as episodes from a single drama. With their narrative power and continuous settings, they seem to constitute a novel in oils.

Horace Walpole

When Israel's King David was old and stricken in years, so the First Book of Kings tells us, his servants brought him a young virgin, Abishag the Shunammite, to 'lie in his bosom so that our lord the king may get heat'. 'And,' the chronicle continues, 'the damsel was very fair, and cherished the king, and ministered to him: but the king knew her not.' Transposed to the eighteenth century, this warming tale exactly applies to the ageing Horace Walpole, who had not one but two Abishags, the charming sisters Mary and Agnes Berry.

Walpole's delicious letters to the Misses Berry were written during the last eight years of life, when he was an old man – very old for the day: he was in his seventies – but still full of charm and intellectual vigour. The Berry sisters were the delight of his declining years; he was more than half in love with them both, and stopped himself proposing to Mary, the elder, only by thinking what people would say if a lifelong bachelor espoused a girl in her twenties. 'When an ancient gentleman marries,' he wrote to them, 'it is his best excuse, that he wants a nurse; which I suppose was the motive of Solomon, who was the wisest of mortals, and a most puissant and opulent monarch, for marrying a thousand wives in his old age, when I conclude he was very gouty. I in humble imitation of that sapient king, and no mines of Ophir flowing into my exchequer, espoused a couple of helpmates.'

Despite appearances, the friendship was not an unequal one. Walpole was, it is true, rich and famous – and the scion of a house

made great by his Prime Minister father, Sir Robert Walpole –
whereas the Berries were poor and socially obscure. He therefore
patronised them, in the best sense of the term; he gave them
a house in the grounds of his extraordinary Gothic creation,
Strawberry Hill, and left them well provided in his will. But the
sisters had much to offer in return. They spoke French fluently,
and read Latin. They had travelled, and knew France and Italy
almost as well as Walpole himself. They were cultured, intelligent, unpretentious and affectionate. After Walpole's death
Mary served as his literary executor, producing the first complete edition of his works. Her journals and letters are one of
the chief sources of information about his life.

Walpole's letters to the Berrys is not just valuable but perhaps
essential to our understanding of him. He is an important figure
in the intellectual history of eighteenth-century England; his
celebrated Gothic novel, *The Castle of Otranto* – highly praised
by Sir Walter Scott and roundly damned by Hazlitt – is the
starting-point of English romanticism. His memoirs of the political life of his times are an invaluable historical document, for
although he was inveterately hostile to his father's political
enemies, he was fair in reporting Parliamentary debates and
personalities, of which – as a silently observing MP for over a
quarter of a century – he had intimate knowledge.

But Walpole's chief contribution to literature is the epistle.
He passionately admired the letters of the seventeenth-century
Madame de Sévigny, who had revived the classical tradition of
letter-writing as a civilised accomplishment. In more than three
thousand letters spanning a period of sixty years Walpole took
the epistolary art to new heights. His chief correspondents
included Sir Horace Mann, long-time British resident of Italy;
the Milton scholar William Cole; the Countess of Ossory; his
old friend Henry Seymour Conway; and the redoubtable Parisian
salon hostess, blind Madame du Deffand (who, when told of the
miracle of St Denis – alleged to have picked up his chopped-off

head and walked 200 kilometres to Paris – tartly remarked, 'In such cases only the first step is difficult').

But in his charming letters to the Berry sisters Walpole is at his most domestic, even at times at his most vulnerable, as when the sisters made a channel-crossing on a night of storms, and Walpole haunted the Gothic gloom of Strawberry Hill in terror for their lives. The letters are unbuttoned, fond, playful, gallant and doting. They glance at great events of the day – the trial of Warren Hastings, the storming of the Bastille and the early days of the French Revolution – giving them an extraordinary freshness and immediacy, reminding one how sharp history's realities were for contemporaries.

And in return we see the life of the Misses Berry, as for example Agnes's aspirations in painting and Mary's crushing disappointments in love, reflected in the mirror of Walpole's concern. In all their lightness and immediacy Walpole's letters are a human testament, witnessing to what he calls in one of them 'the grace of friendship' – words which the editor of his letters aptly used as their collective title.

RIGHTS AND LIBERTIES

Introduction

The essays that follow were written in response to particular circumstances at a particular time. They are defences of civil liberties against the ill-judged action of the British government – mimicking the United States government and others, including the Australian government – in introducing civil-liberty-reducing laws as a supposed defence against the acts of Islamist terrorism that changed perceptions in the early years of the twenty-first century.

These moves by Western governments were a response to the terrorist atrocities now known to history as '9/11', marking the date 11 September 2001 when Islamist terrorists hijacked and then crashed civilian airliners into the World Trade Centre in New York and the Pentagon in Washington. The belief that the West was under siege from, and at war with, Islamist terrorism was strengthened by the Madrid train bombings and the London transport bombings that followed in 2004 and 2005 respectively. Already there had been other terrorist atrocities, pre-dating 9/11, in Nairobi and the Middle East; not least the chronic violence of the Palestinian-Israeli conflict. Together it seemed to many in the West that out of the otherwise peaceful world of Islam was growing a revolting cancer of indiscriminate murderous violence touched with all the lunacy of religious fanaticism.

Moreover, the nature of that terrorism, perpetrated as it was by acts of suicide, prompted a reconsideration of how it was to be anticipated and combated. This fact, more than most, explains the wrong steps that some Western governments next took in domestic policing policy.

Instead of seeing 9/11 and the other atrocities for what they were, namely, criminal acts of mass murder, the American and some other Western governments, saliently including the British government, chose to speak of them in the rhetoric of war. This in particular well served the purposes of those in charge in Washington at the time, who wished to alter the balance of things in the Middle East by conventional military means. But it also gave an excuse to these same governments to alter the balance between the capacity for action of their home policing and security services, and the legal protections and civil liberties long enjoyed by their home populations.

The following essays appeared in newspapers, and one of them – the extended argument against the British government's proposal to introduce identity cards – was a pamphlet issued by the civil liberties organisation Liberty. I have left them in their original form, tied to the circumstances of their production, as part of the record of the time and the debate. What is at stake in them, however, is perennial; and there is great value in showing how perennial issues take vivid point from particular historical circumstances.

Free speech

L aws made in haste as a reaction to perceived crises tend to be bad laws. They can overturn in a hurry what has been achieved through centuries of political and legal endeavour, and they typically prove very resistant to repeal even after maturer reflection has demonstrated their folly.

A classic case is the 1911 Official Secrets Act, passed in a rush in a one-day sitting of Parliament after the 'Agadir Incident' in which Germany forced France to cede the Congo to it, threatening British interests in Africa. Badly drafted and badly thought out, the Act caused immense difficulties for decades before it was replaced in 1989.

Prompted by the upswell of anxiety over terrorism following the 9/11 outrages in the United States, and further prompted by the outrages both committed and attempted in London in the summer of 2005, the British government's legislative initiatives on identity cards, 'incitement to religious hatred', the outlawing of 'glorification' of terrorism, powers to detain suspected terrorists for up to three months, and associated measures, aim at giving the security forces a stronger hand in their response to terrorist threats. All these measures are of exactly the hasty reactive type that does so much harm to civil liberties, which count among the fundamental principles of our free society – and this, note, despite the immediate reaction of Britain's Prime Minister to the '7/7' outrages, when he said that 'the terrorists will not force us to change our ways'.

It should by now be a commonplace, though alas it is not,

that the right response to attempts by violent enemies to coerce our society is to reassert the very liberties and values that make them attack us in the first place. To restrict ourselves out of fear of what they might do is to give them the victory they seek. If they were able to impose their will on our society, they would deprive us of many of the liberties distinctive of a Western democracy. Why do it to ourselves?

Here is an oddity of the situation. The terrorists responsible for the atrocities of 9/11 in New York and Washington, the Madrid train bombings and the London bombings are known to be Muslims and to be inspired by radical Islamist views. The government's proposed new illiberal laws are not, however, aimed only at the Muslim community, from among whom the terrorists are known to come. To do this would seem to be unduly provocative and discriminatory. So the government proposes to place the entire population of the United Kingdom under these illiberal laws, failing to see that if it would be a bad thing to subject a small portion of the population to them, it is considerably worse to make them indiscriminate.

Another oddity is that whereas a previous British government – the coalition under Churchill during the Second World War – introduced illiberal legislation *as a temporary measure* when an entire invasion army was massing on the French coast just twenty miles from our shores, with their aircraft daily bombing us, Britain's present government, faced with a far smaller and more intermittent threat, proposes to reduce our liberties *permanently*.

Both these oddities add up to the government's proposals being radically disproportionate. They are driven by the supposed convenience of the security services, and not at all by issues of principle; which is yet a further worry, because when one discusses these matters with Parliamentarians from both Houses, one is told that the only arguments that will weigh with the government in its pursuit of this legislation are arguments of cost and practicality. In the ID-card case, the soaring costs and the impracticality of the scheme are indeed proving to be the major safeguard of our liberties. In the case of free speech, the government's desire to appease domestic Muslim sensibilities by the inexpensive but drastically ill-advised means of an 'incitement to religious hatred' law has no such safeguard in the offing.

But the question of principle is by far the most important one, and it has to be insisted on loudly and repeatedly, if only – at the very least – so that future generations of well-judging folk can see that we were not all, in this vexed age, unprincipled and rash in our thinking about how to meet the difficulties we face. For there is no question but that there are indeed difficulties. Not all people who value the hard-won liberties of the 'free world' are soft on terrorism or those who plan it and incite it – far from it. Their contempt for people who will use mass murder as an instrument for furthering their views is as boundless as anyone else's, and so is their determination to oppose it.

But they do not plan to oppose it by locking themselves up, by giving away what generations of our own people have won by incremental means over centuries. They do not propose to defeat it by surrendering what most matters to societies like ours: our liberties, not least among them the freedom of speech.

Terrorism and 'incitement to religious hatred'

Neither the government nor the security services have ever claimed that it is possible to prevent terrorist atrocities altogether. Everyone recognises that policing by itself can only be part of the solution. The main part has to be an engagement with the causes of terrorism, both to remove the reasons for it, and in the meantime to isolate terrorists from the support, tacit and otherwise, they get from their communities.

Because the British government assumes, with justification, that today's terrorism stems almost exclusively from disaffection in the Islamic world, it has aimed its domestic counterterrorism strategy at making Britain's own 1.6 million Muslims more at home, in the hope of rendering it inhospitable to both foreign and home-grown radicalism.

The blueprint for this strategy is Operation Contest, adopted by the government in 2005. Its hearts-and-minds thrust includes funding for moderate Islamic news media, encouragement of Muslim interest-exempt banking facilities, and recommendations to companies to make prayer rooms available for Muslim employees. It also includes the controversial proposal currently before Parliament to criminalise 'incitement to religious hatred'.

All of these proposals are well-meaning, and some are positive. But the proposed law against incitement to religious hatred is a serious mistake. Intended as a reassuring gesture towards a small minority, it represents a drastic step towards limiting freedom of expression for the entire population – which is far too high a cost to pay.

Apart from the United States, most countries have laws criminalising offences against religion. In the West such laws have been dead letters in the last hundred years and more, because the opposing value of free speech has been regarded as far outweighing them. But there are sudden danger signals in secular Europe now, warning of a reversal in this arrangement. One indication is that the government's 'religious hatred' law is being proposed just as an Italian magistrate is invoking an old statute criminalising 'vilification of religion' to indict a journalist for offending Islam. She faces two years in prison.

The fact that religion-protecting laws threaten free speech is so obvious that the advocates of Britain's proposed statute are careful to insist that it has inbuilt free-speech safeguards. They claim that satire and criticism directed at religion will not result in prison sentences, because the law aims to protect people not beliefs, and because the Director of Public Prosecutions will have a veto over proposed indictments to ensure that the law is not abused.

Are such reassurances satisfactory? Laws can change in the light of circumstance, so in harsher times this law can easily be refocused to 'protect' against much vaguer provocations, such as 'offence' or 'derogatory remarks'. Consider the similarity of certain laws in present-day Pakistan to those of medieval Europe in this respect. A Pakistani statute of 1984 specifies life imprisonment or death for utterance of 'derogatory remarks' about the Koran. The country's Federal Sharia Court additionally ruled in 1990 that 'the penalty for contempt of the Holy Prophet . . . is death and nothing else'. This resembles laws protecting Christianity in earlier phases of European history, when the cognate crimes of heresy and blasphemy were capital offences. As this shows, history has a bad habit of repeating itself in different places and guises, especially if a door is left ajar for it to do so.

The Italian journalist currently in trouble is Oriana Fallaci, one of her country's most controversial because often least temperate writers. Following 9/11 she assumed the role of defender of Western values against Islamic assaults upon them. The occasion for her indictment is a book in which, among other things, she laments what she sees as a deliberate 'invasion' of Europe by Muslim immigrants, who she says intend to efface European culture and identity.

In support of these claims she cites a speech made by Algerian President Houari Boumédienne at the UN in 1974: 'One day millions of men will leave the southern hemisphere to go to the northern hemisphere. And they will not go there as friends. Because they will go there to conquer it. And they will conquer it with their sons. The wombs of our women will give us victory.' And she quotes a Catholic bishop who heard a Muslim cleric tell Westerners at an interfaith meeting in Turkey, 'Thanks to your democratic laws we will invade you. Thanks to our Islamic laws we will conquer you.'

Most of Fallaci's anger is reserved for the failure of Europe to recognise what she sees as the current realisation of these threats. Her response to 9/11, the blunt language she uses in criticising 'the sons of Allah' and in asserting the superiority of European liberalism over Islamic culture, has provoked an Islamist activist in Italy, one Adel Smith (an Egyptian-Scottish Muslim immigrant), to lay a complaint against her under the 'vilification of religion' law. Ironically, Smith is himself on indictment under the same law, for abusing Catholicism; and is well known in Italy for provocative activities – demanding that crucifixes be removed from schools and hospitals, and allegedly calling for Oriana Fallaci to be 'exterminated'.

The Fallaci case illustrates the danger posed by laws protecting faiths and their votaries. In circumstances where tensions are provoked by assertive identity politics based on faith affiliation, such laws provide ready weapons for all sides to attack each other in court. It is a short step from the court-room to riots in the streets outside. Rhetoric matters in such cases; if someone is indicted for disturbing the peace rather than specifically causing 'religious' offence, there is far less rationale for faith groups to gather outside courtrooms bran-dishing sticks.

Britain already has laws protecting citizens from verbal or physical attack, no matter how motivated. A current Met-ropolitan Police leaflet, printed in no fewer than eleven lan-guages, asks: 'Have you ever been abused or attacked because of your race, your religion, the colour of your skin, or your sexual orientation?' And it tells readers that the police can protect anyone thus abused, 'if appropriate by arresting' those responsible. That is unequivocal: threatening behaviour, assault and battery have always been crimes, whatever provokes them. No new crime needs to be invented.

The Fallaci case shows why inventing a new crime would be profoundly misguided. At this juncture in history, when a new clash is occurring – or rather, being deliberately engineered – between the secular arrangements of European liberal dem-ocracies and some increasingly assertive religious groups within them, the need for free speech, however abrasive and chal-lenging, is more important than ever. Religious radicals want to limit our freedoms; to curb free speech is to give them exactly what they want. The worst-case scenario is that what will come from limiting free speech is, in the end, silence.

No one is a Christian or Muslim at birth; people are made so by the community they are born into, or which they later join. They can choose not to be Christian or Muslim, and can convert to another faith or none. But they cannot choose to be other than ethnically white or black. Ultimately, membership of a religious group is a voluntary matter – even if the coercive effects of childhood brain-washing and social pressure makes opting out difficult. This puts all religions on the same footing as political parties or other voluntary organisations: they are self-selected interest groups, defined by belief or aim, artificial constructs dependent on personal conviction. No one could tolerate the idea that members of a political party should be protected by law against satire or criticism; by the same token neither should a religion and its members.

This especially matters now, because the major religions are busily engaged in pushing themselves further into the public domain, demanding more privileges and protections than they have enjoyed for a long time. The vacuum left by the Cold War's end has been filled by increasing Islamist militancy premised on hostility to a materialist West which the militants' leaders blame for their problems. The other major religions, not wishing to be left behind in the assertiveness stakes, make common cause with them, demanding public money for faith-based schools (the dreadful consequences of which are seen to this day in Northern Ireland), faith representation in the House of Lords, new laws protecting believers qua believers, and much besides.

This common cause can only be temporary, because each of the faiths lays claim to final truth, and they blaspheme one another therefore; so that deep traditional conflicts are merely waiting their time to re-emerge, something far more likely to happen if the religions have been given a larger slice of the public domain, and protection for their special-interest activities there.

Whether or not one agrees with Oriana Fallaci's views – and despite the fact that it is not always easy to condone the manner in which they are put – her indictment is a portent for Britain and all Europe in this climate. It represents secularism and free speech under pressure, indeed under threat: and passing laws to give self-described believers protection from both secularism and free speech increases that pressure, and promises ultimately to turn the threat into reality.

In freedom's name: the case against identity cards

All we have of freedom, all we use or know,
This our fathers bought for us long and long ago.

So they bought us freedom – not at little cost;
Wherefore we must watch the King, lest our gain be lost.

He shall mark our goings, question where we came,
Set his guards about us, as in freedom's name.

He shall peep and mutter, and the night shall bring
Watchers 'neath our window, lest we mock the King.

Rudyard Kipling

PREFACE

In what follows I argue that the idea of an identity-card scheme is wrong in principle and will be an expensive failure in practice. Its only concrete effect will be to undermine the traditional liberties of British citizens, almost certainly irreversibly. In

Australia the proposal for an ID card was rejected in 1987 by a public which had at first accepted the idea, only to become averse when it understood the issues more clearly – issues of civil liberties and cost. In this essay I add a voice to all those that have so eloquently sought to enlighten political and public opinion in the same way.

In Part I I put a polemical case against the principle of ID cards; in Part II I examine the question of practicalities and their implications, chiefly by addressing the evidence that was given to the Home Affairs Committee of the House of Commons before the General Election of May 2005. This evidence was overwhelming in its strength of objection to an ID-card system, a fact not reflected in the Committee's subsequent report, nor taken into account by the Home Office in insisting on pressing ahead with the scheme nevertheless.

The Home Affairs Committee almost wholly left aside the deep questions of principle involved, in particular as relating to the damage done to civil liberties, on the grounds that these were discussed in connection with earlier proposals to introduce ID cards, e.g. in 1995–6, and it concentrated mainly on the practical question of effectiveness and cost. These latter are thought to be the principal grounds that will defeat the ID-card proposals. I shall state that case; but I am dismayed that even the many opponents of the proposal in Parliament do not feel that the questions of principle can weigh with those eager to see ID cards introduced. This is a deeply troubling consideration, especially for those who in other respects might wish the government well.

Having read both the evidence given to the Home Affairs Committee and the Committee's subsequent report, I find myself astonished that the overwhelming weight of evidence showing that an ID-card scheme will be extremely expensive and largely ineffective was not properly reflected in the Committee's report. I say this with due respect to the

Committee and its members, some of whom, during the examination of witnesses, asked some very pertinent questions indeed; for doubtless the great eagerness of the Home Office to introduce an ID-card scheme resulted in the report not being an accurate reflection of the profound reservations of the majority of the witnesses who appeared before it. (By 'Home Office' here I mean its politicians; almost all its civil servants are emphatically against the idea.) Officials involved in the drafting of the report bear regrettable private witness to this fact too; but the discrepancy between the weight of evidence given to the Committee, and the conclusions it drew, speaks for itself.[i]

Part I: Polemics

Volunteer or conscript?

Our great poet John Milton was travelling in Italy when he heard the news that civil war had broken out in his homeland. He immediately began preparations to return. 'I considered it base,' he wrote a few years later, 'that while my fellow-countrymen were fighting at home for liberty, I should be travelling at my ease for intellectual culture.'[ii] There seem, alas, to be no Miltons today for the defence of liberty in Britain, though a mind and pen like his are as necessary now as they were when he lived, given that preserving the freedoms won for us by our forebears, with such difficulty over so many centuries, is a constant challenge. But we can at least take our cue from him, and set aside ordinary avocations when presented with the possibility of a fundamentally negative change in our relationship to the state of which we are citizens, a change that diminishes our individual liberty by making us conscripts rather than volunteers in our own land. This is what the increasingly necessary and finally obligatory possession of identity cards will do, and that is why it is so important to understand why an ID-card scheme should not be accepted.

It is not a matter of theory and politics only that drives the sense of urgency in what follows. I have lived and worked in countries where each individual had to have a pass-book or an identity card and to present them to the authorities when required. My parents, like most of the parents of those reading these words, accepted the privations and duties of the Second World War because, like all their fellow British citizens, they did not want the Gestapo on the streets of London and Manchester, Cardiff and Glasgow, asking to see people's 'papers'. But the principle that was defended then is disregarded now, in the deeply mistaken belief that the introduction of a system of ID cards is a merely bureaucratic measure which will make life more difficult for illegal immigrants and 'identity thieves', while also in some unspecified and vague way helping to deter terrorism and crime.

The thought of being obliged to possess a document encoding one's personal details for inspection on demand by the authorities is a profoundly disagreeable one, so contrary is it to the traditional independence, privacy and liberty of British citizens. The further idea that this document connects with information kept on a 'National Identity Register', centrally maintained by government, is even worse. It is a surprise that the very phrase *National Identity Register* does not appal a population whose history in the last eight hundred years has been distinguished by pride in possessing important liberties – liberties denied, for the greater part of that time, to most of the rest of mankind.

I have seen people queuing at a desk while officials peruse their papers – not at a border, not while abroad in a foreign country, but in the middle of their own home towns; and not because they were under suspicion, or asking for anything from a public agency, but because they were being checked. Being checked! – what an innocuous phrase, but how freighted with the implication that each such individual is not a free member of a free society, but a conscript in a system of suspicion and surveillance.

For that, when understood frankly and without the mask of rhetoric, is what ID cards are: they are devices of surveillance. They should therefore be called 'individual surveillance cards' or 'individual tracking cards', or 'tagging cards' or even perhaps 'policing surveillance tags'. In campaigns of opposition in other countries they have been given the names 'internal passports' or 'licences to live'. Whatever sobriquet comes to stick to them, an ID card is an instrument of policing by central authority, and it is this fact about them that breaches fundamental considerations of civil liberty.

One immediate standard defence of ID cards is that we already have so many identity-encoding documents in the form of credit cards, store cards, passports, driving licences and the rest, that one more – and moreover one that tidies all these diverse documents into one – is scarcely a problem. The answer is simple. We can leave aside the fact that the last part of this claim is demonstrably false. Many countries have ID cards, and suffer as much if not more crime and terrorism as does the UK; this is an argument that has long since been lost by proponents of ID cards.[iii] Rather, the point is that to think that having ID cards is not different from having these other identifying documents is to make a deep mistake. Credit cards, passports and driving licences are documents we *choose* to have. We do not have to have them; our possession of them is voluntary, even though the convenience of them for their purposes is such that in practical terms it is at very least a great nuisance (and in the case of not having a passport, a limitation) to do without them. But there is an immense difference of principal between (a) choosing to enter a relationship with banks, with retail companies, with the vehicle licensing authority, and with whoever else issues us with a document specific to the purpose for which we choose to have it, and (b) *being obliged by law* to have a document that encodes our personal information for use by central authorities. To be obliged – required, forced by law – to have such a document is to be a conscript in a system, whether one wishes it or no.

It is this change – from volunteer to conscript – which is the change that ID cards intrinsically represent, and this is a fundamental diminution of our liberty as individuals. The reason why this is so is made clear in the discussion to come. First, though, it is essential to ask and answer the question, 'Who benefits most from the introduction of ID cards?' because part of the reason why ID cards are such an attack on liberty lies in the answer.

Who benefits?

The three main beneficiaries of an ID-card scheme, if one were introduced, would be the police, criminals, and the biometric data companies which have devised the technology for encoding identifying information onto a card. Consideration of how each of these three groups would benefit proves illuminating.

The police and security services would benefit because an ID card is designed to function as a number plate does on a motor vehicle – as a convenient means for the authorities to identify the owner, and to keep track of the vehicle – which in the ID case means the person himself. The sole difference is that an ID card would contain much more information than the police can currently get by looking up a vehicle registration number; all that this latter mainly provides is the name and address of the owner, and by extension (once these details are known) whether he or she has a criminal record. By giving people their own number plates – an ID card – the police can keep track of them just as they can track a motor car, and can call up information just as they can when they radio a vehicle registration number to central control – with ID cards yielding far more information.

Now, the number-plate analogy should strike a dispassionate observer as an uncomfortable one, especially if one thinks into the future, and asks about the convergence of technological developments with practicalities. Suppose that it comes to be standard that each individual must by law have an ID card – that is, a number plate like a car – that the authorities can check up, and without which an individual cannot have a job and cannot access any goods and services (the original idea of ID cards as 'entitlement cards' was explained by the then Home Secretary as at least meaning that no one could be employed or get medical services, etc., without them[iv]). One can imagine circumstances such as obtained in wartime when perhaps people cannot move around one's country or even town without an ID card. This is not currently projected for the UK, but how quickly things change when the means exist, as other countries show.

In this circumstance it will quickly become apparent that having an ID *card* will be inconvenient, for ID cards can and will be lost, or stolen, or forged. In the interests of practicality the German government of 1932–45 found it convenient to keep track of some classes of people by burning an identifying number onto their arms, but in our more sophisticated times the great advantage of nanotechnology – already with us – will offer a different solution: a very tiny chip, less than the size of a full-stop on this page, will be easily and painlessly inserted in an ear-lobe or under the skin of the wrist, carrying all the personal and biometric information that the authorities would need for a secure identification. We already have machines that can access such encoded information – the laser guns that read barcodes in supermarkets provide a direct analogy –

so it is a short step to having machines that can pick up and read information from implanted subcutaneous nanochips – there by law, remember – wherever we go in our towns and country.

It might seem a good idea to put traceable number plates on criminals and terrorists so that they can be tracked and monitored by the police. But however many terrorists, fraudsters, drug traffickers and other criminals there are – let us overstate the case and suggest that, as there are 60,000 of them in our prisons, and supposing that we only catch one in a hundred, there are therefore half a million bad people in our society – it is excessive to brand with number plates, as all the victims of Nazism were branded with number plates, all 60 million of us in order to curb the activities of 1 per cent of us. And not just vastly excessive, but an insult to the non-criminal and non-terrorist 99 per cent of us, and worse still a deprivation of our individual liberty resulting from the monitoring and tracking to which we would be subject as tagged conscripts of the state.

The first group of people who will benefit from an ID-card scheme, then, will be the police and security authorities; it is a godsend for them, bringing them all and more of the benefits of motor-vehicle registration plates. They are not, therefore, concerned by the idea of turning people into traceable numbered entities, and in their submission to the Home Affairs Committee they (along with the potential commercial beneficiaries of the scheme) were most enthusiastic for it.

The second group of people who will benefit from ID cards and their forthcoming more sophisticated versions will be criminals themselves, or at least those among them dedicated to selling forged identities and doctored biometrics on cards and nanochips. Think of the disastrous era of Prohibition in the United States, when the sale and consumption of alcohol was banned. The result of this ill-conceived law was the creation of an immense criminal industry dedicated to circumventing the law in every way. The absorption of police time and the internecine warfare of the gangs that sprang up to take advantage of the new opportunities thus presented did infinitely more harm to society than was ever done by the consumption of alcohol before Prohibition. Criminality inspired by the introduction of ID cards will show closely similar patterns.

Criminals are the paradigms of entrepreneurs. Once identity becomes an invaluable commodity which by law everyone must have and of necessity be able to prove, the fraternity of thieves, forgers and fraudsters will have a golden opportunity to profit. Some will become expert in stealing ID cards, others in adapting them, yet others in forging them outright. There is almost nothing that cannot be stolen, and almost nothing that cannot be forged enough to fool some of the people some of the time, and on these facts will be based the criminal industry that would result from the introduction of ID cards.

But the greatest gainers by far – to the tune of many billions of pounds, together with unending revenues stretching into the future: for every year many people will be born, and many others will lose their cards or have them stolen – will be the biometric data companies. Hereby hangs a very particular tale, for it is the biometric data companies which, in company with the police, are pushing the government hardest for the introduction of ID cards, since they stand to gain so much from them.

If ID cards were simply bits of paper containing a photograph and the bearer's name and address, they would be of no use to anyone. But the availability of the technology for encoding biometric data – fingerprints, iris and facial patterns – is what makes them seem plausible to governments and security services, as a result of the vigorous marketing that the manufacturers of such technology have conducted.

A classic instance of an analogous commercially driven assault on civil liberties is the production by pharmaceutical companies of easy-to-use drug-testing kits, which such companies market to businesses by saying, 'Have you considered your legal liabilities if one of your staff is under the influence of drugs, and as a result causes harm or loss to a client?' Of course, drug-testing of employees by companies might be desirable in the case of airline pilots and chauffeurs, but it is in most other cases an unwarranted invasion of privacy. Given that testing kits can reveal whether employees have made recreational use of drugs during a preceding weekend, and given that most occupations are not thereby affected, it is obvious that if a company is persuaded by pharma-marketing to buy and use such kits, it is committing a gross violation of its employees' privacy.

The case with biometric ID cards is exactly similar. Companies like NEC and Precise Biometrics are vigorously marketing identification technologies to governments, and the potential rewards are enormous. The cost of introducing ID cards in the UK is currently given as at least £5.5 billion (according to many reports, this is a major underestimate: the latest figure at time of writing, given by the *Financial Times* and in a detailed study by the London School of Economics, is £18 billion), at a cost of between a hundred and several hundred pounds to each individual – a recurring cost, for lost and stolen cards and for changes of information requiring to be encoded. The biggest slice of this enormous sum will go to companies supplying the biometric technology to be included in the cards. All of it will be paid by individual citizens.

In light of these potential commercial rewards, the biometric technology companies are not concerned about privacy and civil liberties. On the NEC website the company proudly announces that its biometric identification products 'facilitate highly accurate identity and security processes, without the need for contact or interaction with the person being identified'. Precise Biometrics equally proudly announces that its products 'can be built into almost any device'. The promise held out by these statements is that a civilian population can be surveyed, tracked and monitored twenty-four hours a day, without its knowledge, or with it knowing only that it is under general surveillance.

To some extent this is already happening in the UK, which has more CCTV cameras in operation than any other country in the world. But these cameras monitor public space, and in effect take the place of policemen on the beat there, helping to deter crime or at least to alert the police to its occurrence, and not infrequently helping to identify criminals. For these reasons it can be justified. But the kind of complete biometric surveillance made possible by what NEC and Precise Biometrics offer is a quite different thing: it is greatly more far-reaching, invasive and personal.

The fact that biometric technology companies are a driving-force behind the government's plans to introduce ID cards has not been a factor in the public debate about them because so far it has not been publicly recognised. But it should be, because as motivations go for major changes in the constitutional status of individual citizens it is a very bad one, and needs to be contested. So it is important to note that if it were not for the biometric technology companies, there would be no question of ID cards; simple paper or plastic cards with a photo and an address would be so open to fraud that no government would now bother with them. But iris, fingerprint and face-recognition technology appear (as it happens, incorrectly; but that is another and equally long story) to offer secure identification control, and that is why ID cards are on the agenda.

In the different field of advances in medical technology, which throw up increasingly vexed ethical questions about life, death, fertility, birth, cloning and the use of embryos in medical research and treatment, there is now quite rightly an informed public debate about whether 'we can' implies 'we should'. In the case of ID cards, we have not even begun to connect the 'we can' factor – 'we can offer biometric identification technologies,' say the commercial suppliers of them – with the 'we should' question. It is essential that we do.

Justification or rationalisation?

The proponents of ID cards invoke the rhetoric of controlling illegal immigration and fighting a 'war on crime', and likewise a 'war on terror', as justifications for the introduction of ID cards. Times of actual or perceived crisis have always been used by governments as a reason for increasing their central powers and limiting citizens' freedoms. Sometimes this is justified, as in the Second World War, on the understanding that the increased powers and diminished liberties are *temporary*, to last for the period of crisis only. What is now proposed is a *permanent* increase in central power and correlative loss of liberties.

In fact the drive to introduce ID cards puts one in mind of the reactionary administrations of Pitt the Younger and Lord Liverpool in the decades between 1790 and 1820, when habeas corpus was suspended, nascent trade unions and 'corresponding societies' banned, and taxes on paper raised to prevent information getting to working people, ostensibly to counter the revolutionary threat from France but also useful in stifling the growing reform movements of the eighteenth century.

But even Pitt had the justification of war with a potent adversary; there is no justification for the present attacks on civil liberties either in the United Kingdom or the United States. In the latter the Patriot Act (a name painfully redolent of Orwell's Newspeak) has given powers to government security agencies which, if the fear-inducing rhetoric of a supposed 'war on terror' were not distracting the public, would be seen for what they are: major invasions of privacy and diminutions of individual rights. They license 'sneak and peek' activities by security services, sequestration of assets on grounds that would not be permitted as evidence in US courts, and availability of draconian emergency powers to State governors.

Yet even in the United States the Federal government has stated that it will not to go so far as to introduce a national ID card, precisely because of the civil liberty implications. And it was these latter that made the Australian people, through a massive public campaign, force its government to drop a proposed ID-card law in 1987.

The idea of liberty

What is at stake with the proposed introduction of ID cards is a fundamental diminution of individual liberty. 'Liberty' is a complex concept with a history, and requires clarification. Its root meaning is the condition of being free from restrictions which either prevent people from acting in ways of their own choosing, or which force them to act in ways not of their own choosing. In circumstances where liberty is thus curtailed, the restriction also typically aims to make people think or believe in ways conformable to the restrictors' own, but since this is difficult to achieve, restrictors of liberty take the second best course of attempting to block access to information or opinions that might lead people to adopt unacceptable views – the restrictors' fear being that such views will eventually lead to action contrary to what the restrictors want.

The correlative to this root meaning is liberty as the power for – and in modern times we would add the right or the immunity of – people to act and speak as they choose. It is obvious that in the interests of peaceful and co-operative societies and the individuals in them, liberty in both these related senses cannot be unfettered; we could not tolerate a situation now – and such situations once were the rule – in which a stronger person could use his strength to dominate, dispossess, rape, enslave or otherwise maltreat weaker people, without the latter having any protection. This is how aristocracies and royal houses began; their power and wealth was thereafter retained by institutionalising the gains that strength had once wrested from everyone else. The rule of law, and the existence of laws, aims precisely at guarding against this injustice. They protect the interests of all by placing agreed limits on liberty. Thinkers in early modern times such as Thomas Hobbes, John Locke and Jean-Jacques Rousseau represented this arrangement as a 'social contract' in which everyone sacrifices part of their individual sovereignty in return for the benefits and protection afforded by society.

But the implicitly voluntary yielding of part of individual liberty for the benefits of social membership is not a limitless or unconscious thing. Once a society has matured to the point where the 'contract' is something everyone understands and can debate, discussion of the question of which liberties are to be restricted in the interests of the whole, and under what conditions, becomes a central part of the political process. This leads to the third and most conspicuously contemporary sense of 'liberty', as *freedom from unjust or undue government control; as immunity from the arbitrary exercise of authority.*

This third aspect of liberty is the crucial one for present purposes. In the debate a society has with itself about how it can best be organised and protected, the key point is the nature and extent of the laws aimed at achieving this. And one central question here is always whether, when such laws involve an encroachment on individual liberty, that encroachment is just, necessary and proportionate. That is the test that has to be applied to the case of identity cards. Each of the three terms 'just', 'necessary' and 'proportionate' has full weight in this.

The question of the justice of imposing an obligation on

individuals to have an instrument to prove who they are when required to do so, is a question of principle, and relates to the fundamental question of what sort of society we take ours to be.

The question of whether there is a genuine necessity for imposing such an obligation on individuals is a question of practicality. It involves measuring what the authorities, and individuals themselves, gain from having everyone under an obligation to possess an identity card, against the risks and dangers that such possession is supposed to avoid or lessen.

The question of the proportionality or appropriateness of a national identity-card scheme is one that combines both the question of principle and the question of practicality. If the authorities impose an obligation on everyone to possess an identity card, this is certainly a diminution of individual liberty, but is it an undue one?

The answer obviously depends on circumstances. In the Second World War, the British government required citizens to carry ID cards because a formidable enemy army was massing twenty miles from the coast with the intention of invading, and its air arm was daily attacking targets on British soil. As definitions of 'clear and present danger' go, this is a paradigm; and in taking every precaution to defend against the imminence of disastrous attack, a raft of restrictions on individual liberties was introduced, of which the imposition of ID cards was one. In such a case restrictions on peacetime liberties cannot be seen as undue, for the circumstances were not merely undue but extremely dangerous. In the years after the war ended the liberties were restored, the abolition of ID cards being one of the acts in their restoration, on the grounds that maintaining the restrictions was no longer appropriate.[v]

In the present debate, the point to be determined is whether the circumstances are anywhere near equivalent to having Hitler's Wehrmacht and Panzers massing on the French coast, and hundreds of Luftwaffe bombers attacking Britain daily. That kind of circumstance justified the *temporary* introduction of ID cards; our question of proportionality is: are current circumstances, today in 2005, such that they warrant the *permanent* introduction of ID cards? Do we live in a time of danger equal to or greater than the threatened Nazi invasion of 1940?

Autonomy, sovereignty, independence

Every concept belongs to a family of closely related concepts, and one good way of grasping a concept's full import is by taking note of the other members of its family. Thus, the concept of liberty belongs with the concepts *of freedom, emancipation, autonomy, independence, self-determination* and *sovereignty.* Any diminution of liberty is a diminution of these others too. The history of liberty in Europe and the European-influenced world since the early sixteenth century – that is, since the Reformation – is the history of increasing individual autonomy achieved by emancipation from the hegemony of a single religious authority, from absolute monarchy, from serfdom and slavery, from illiteracy, and from unjust laws which the majority had no hand in framing and which they could not repudiate. Each step in this emancipation enlarged the sphere in which the individual could be – to speak without metaphor – his own monarch.

In the quarter of the world where this degree of individual independence is now a commonplace – the 'Western world' – and where it is therefore taken for granted, people have become ignorant of the real meaning of their liberty. For one example, they have become oblivious to the real import of the fact – extraordinary in human history – that no policeman or other government agent can enter their homes without a warrant from a magistrate, that is, without having first persuaded an independent official that there is genuinely good cause to enter the private domain of a free individual without his permission. In the realms of the Gestapo and behind the Iron Curtain, a knock on the door in the early hours of morning was one palpable sign of the absence of individual liberty. When one ponders this point attentively for a minute or two, one begins to see that liberty is a treasure, a real one, not lightly or lazily to be given up.

'Who I am' is one central feature of the private domain of my liberty. If I am obliged to possess an ID card, I have in effect been presented with a permanent warrant for the authorities to enter that private domain whenever they wish. There is a close relationship between this point and another long-standing protection of the liberty of the individual: the presumption of innocence before the law. This latter says that if the authorities bring charges against an individual, it is up to them to establish the individual's guilt, and not for him to prove his innocence. Mandatory possession of an ID card is analogous to having to prove to the authorities that you are innocent, instead of them having to prove their case against you. It is the expression of a new obligation to reveal to the authorities on their demand who I am, where I live, and whatever other information is carried on the chip on the card or on the 'National Identity Register'. This means that an ID card gives the authorities permanent open access to private facts about me – or, alternatively put, it is the end of privacy about those facts.

This shows how deeply contrary to the evolution of individual liberty the ID-card proposal is. In the thought of John Locke and Jean-Jacques Rousseau, individuals were taken to have natural rights that could never be denied or limited by society, not even in the implicitly voluntary establishment of the 'social contract'. In the American Declaration of Independence these rights were described as 'inalienable'. They were, however, wisely enshrined in the Constitution adopted by the United States, because the idea of 'natural' rights can be debated by those who see rights as acquired in an historical process, beginning in medieval times with guilds of traders and craftsmen, later by the claim of minorities in imperial settings to the use of their own languages and cultures, later still to particular groups establishing a case for special protection or for access to previously denied social goods and opportunities. The claim of women to equal treatment in society is a recent example of rights acquired in the face of historical opposition.

Liberty itself consists of a family of rights, whether natural or acquired: freedom of speech and the press, of association, of conscience, of private judgement in religion, of privacy, of choice whom to marry, and of freedom from oppression and enslavement, unjust and cruel treatment, and discrimination on grounds of race, sex or creed. Most of humankind still lacks most of these aspects of liberty, amazingly – another reason to protect them wherever they exist.

But the bare enumeration of the rights whose enjoyment confers liberty on an individual does not capture the ideal that together they are meant to express: of the autonomous private individual whose personal sphere is his own, and into which he admits others by choice, as in his friendships and affections. He might voluntarily share personal information about his tastes and interests, needs and problems, financial affairs and marital status, and so forth, with a variety of public agencies because he wishes to derive the benefits of engaging with those agencies for some purpose he recognises as good or useful. But the idea that impersonal and unknown parties could at will or on demand access the central facts of his identity without his permission or knowledge is a quite different matter.

This iterates the central and essential point about mandatory ID cards making people conscripts rather than volunteers in their own societies. It is a profoundly sobering thought that to date the only people who live under conscript conditions in our society – that is, such that details of their identity and whereabouts are known to and monitorable (usually, actually monitored) by the authorities – are convicted but released paedophiles, murderers out of prison on licence, and persons suspected of terrorist plotting and drug-trafficking. Since these people are already under identity surveillance, the introduction of ID cards is not especially relevant to their relationship with the authorities; which is doubtless why, when the ID-card bill was revived after the general election of 2005, its main rhetorical justification – a greatly weaker one – had become 'protection against identity fraud'. This latter, however, is a matter for individuals and their banks, credit card and utility companies to guard against, both by technological means and common-sense precautions; ID cards will not make much difference to the absence or presence of security in these fields.

It is a very unattractive proposal that every one of us in our society should be placed in the same class of persons under general surveillance along with convicted paedophiles, murderers out of prison on licence, and suspicious characters monitored by the security services.

'Watchers 'neath our window'

The quotation from Kipling used here as epigraph was quoted in a speech given by E. M. Forster to the Congrès Internationale des Ecrivains at Paris in 1935, when every horizon was darkening with threats, Hitler and Stalin were in power and increasing the size of their armies and armaments, and the international order was falling apart – a situation fraught with far greater horror and menace than exists now. Forster's speech, entitled 'Liberty in England', addressed the question of the then existing threat to liberty in his homeland. He did not regard Sir Oswald Mosley's fascism as a threat, unless the United Kingdom were defeated by Nazi Germany and Mosley was put in charge as Hitler's puppet. Instead, he said, 'we are menaced by something much more insidious – by what I might call "Fabio-Fascism", by the dictator-spirit working quietly away behind the façade of constitutional forms, passing a little law (like the Sedition Act) here, endorsing a departmental tyranny there, emphasising the national need for secrecy elsewhere, and whispering and cooing the so-called "news" every evening over the wireless, until opposition is tamed and gulled. Fabio-Fascism is what I am afraid of, for it is the traditional method by which liberty has been attacked in England. It was the method of King Charles I – a gentleman if ever there was one – the method of our enlightened authoritarian gentlemen today. This Fabio-Fascism is our old enemy, the tyrant:

> 'He shall mark our goings, question whence we came
> Set his guards about us, as in freedom's name.
> He shall peep and mutter, and the night shall bring
> Watchers 'neath our window, lest we mock the King.

' "As in Freedom's name." How well Kipling puts it!'

At the time Forster wrote these words, his concern was prompted by the Sedition Act and the censorship of literature on grounds of obscenity. The latter was a long-standing problem in a country in which prim religious sentiment refused to countenance the frank discussion of human realities, preferring silence and ignorance and the tyranny of disapproval to keep moral order. But the Sedition Act was a typical illiberal response to perceived threat, and one in a woefully long series of such – as with the late and unlamented Official Secrets Act, which was passed in a moment of panic in 1911 because of German threats to British interests in Central Africa, and which thereafter bedevilled British society until it was put to a merciful death not long ago.

The Sedition Act, its passing by Parliament and its purpose contain many useful lessons for observing how illiberal legislation works in our country. 'The most open blow that has lately been struck against freedom of expression in England,' Forster continued, 'is the Sedition Act. ... Its official title is the Incitement to Disaffection Act, and it was passed last year by our so-called National Government by the large majority which is always at its command. This Act restores the right of General Search (condemned as illegal for the last 170 years), it impedes the moral and political education of the soldier, it encourages the informer, and it can be employed against pacifists. There were strong protests against it, which were scarcely reported by the daily Press or by the BBC; the protests were not without effect, and some of the more dangerous clauses in the original Bill were withdrawn while it was in committee. It is the sort of a measure which a government passes in order to have up its sleeve, in the event of an emergency.'[vi]

Note the various points here: the overturning of long-held liberties on the excuse of present emergency, the way that such legislation gets through its Committee stages in Parliament by concessions and adjustments – no doubt the framers of legislation know what to put in that can be taken out without loss to the main purpose – and then the fact that what is said about the new law will assuredly be forgotten or modified in time. As with ID cards, the Home Secretary says that there will be no necessity to carry them always, then that will change and they will have to be producible on demand in the street to a policeman or in a bank or benefits office, and then because of the aforementioned inconvenience of lost and stolen cards, the nanochip will come to be inserted under the skin. So it goes.

Liberators

One would think that anyone who assumed the great office of state of Home Secretary would look back across the landscape of political history, and ask himself or herself the question: how would I like to be remembered? Would I like to be seen as an illiberal, reactionary, liberty-reducing tyrant, or as a Herbert Morrison or Roy Jenkins?

What a contrast to the recent and present Home Office is provided by these latter-named Home Secretaries. Herbert Morrison was Home Secretary during the Second World War, a time of real crisis unlike the present. During the course of the war a committee of campaigners was set up to object to the use of 'area bombing' of civilian targets in Germany, and one of its members, Vera Brittain, wrote a pamphlet called 'Seed of Chaos' setting out the facts and objections to this form of aerial warfare. Most people regarded the committee as subversive and as aiding the Nazis by means of its campaign, and lobbied Morrison to have them put in jail. Morrison replied that they were free citizens entitled to their views and to the statement of them. That is the attitude of a truly liberal and magnanimous mind.

How much more this applies to Roy Jenkins, who in the heady days of the 1960s decriminalised homosexuality, lifted censorship restrictions, abolished the death penalty, reduced the punitive and restrictive nature of divorce laws, and saved thousands of women from the dangers of back-street abortions by providing for legal terminations of pregnancy in the National Health Service. The thinking that lay behind the liberalising regime that Jenkins introduced as Home Secretary is set out in a short book he wrote in 1959 for the Penguin Special series, *The Labour Case*. Its concluding chapter is, in his own words, 'about the need to make this country a more civilized place', and he identifies the first step in doing so as 'the need for the State to do less to restrict personal freedom'.[vii] This was written, remember, in the near-aftermath of McCarthyism in the United States, and even as the Cold War grew in dangerous frostiness, with its very real threat of annihilating nuclear war. Nominating the need to increase personal freedom as the first desideratum of civilising Britain is made all the more interesting by what else Jenkins thought was necessary. 'First, there is the need for the State to do less to restrict personal freedom. Secondly, there is the need for the State to do more to encourage the arts, to create towns which are worth living in, and to preserve a countryside which is worth looking at. Thirdly, there is the need, independently of the State, to create a climate of opinion which is favourable to gaiety, tolerance and beauty, and unfavourable to puritanical restriction, to petty-minded disapproval, to hypocrisy, and to a dreary, ugly pattern of life.'[viii]

The reforms he proceeded to carry out when he came to office a few years later were all prefigured in that chapter, along with some aims that the inherent conservatism of society prevented him from accomplishing. Capital punishment, homosexuality, censorship, Sunday observance laws, licensing hours, betting restrictions, divorce laws, immigration regulations and the law criminalising suicide all, he wrote, had to be liberalised.[ix] Although he was not able to relax Sunday observance and licensing restrictions as much as he wished, and although at least one of the necessary reforms – decriminalising suicide – was carried out by the then Conservative government soon after his book was published, his concerns and his actions in office mark him out as a great reforming Home Secretary, and a courageous one – and as a model to follow for successors who might like to enter the historical record other than as reactionary enemies of liberty.

Mandatory ID cards would be anathema to the likes of E. M. Forster, Herbert Morrison and Roy Jenkins. They would see, and rightly so, the obligation to have a card containing personal information for inspection by the authorities as a long backward step, a de-civilising step. In the great debates that surrounded the independence of former British dependencies in the days of Empire, the argument was often put that the people of the dependencies were as children, insufficiently mature in the ways of civilisation to be trusted with self-government, independence and autonomy. Leave aside the fact that this ignored the millennia of self-government achieved by these peoples before the colonisers arrived, and consider the implications of the idea of political maturity here. If individuals cannot be trusted as free agents, as volunteers in their own societies, but have to be regimented and monitored by possession of mandatory ID cards, they are being as it were infantilised, demoted from the status of sovereign beings, and colonised in their own lands by a system of centralised information and tracking. Forster, Morrison and Jenkins would not entertain such a proposal for one instant.

Machiavelli or muddle-head?

It is an extraordinary development that mandatory ID cards should even be contemplated at the beginning of the twenty-first century in a first world country; and the alternative explanations as to why a government should seek to introduce them are none of them very attractive. One – I think and hope the least likely – is a Machiavellian one, in which (so those of conspiratorial bent might say) a plot is being laid for the eventual Orwellian Big Brother control of increasingly many aspects of individual lives. Although this is not the probable intention, the reality is that as time goes by something a bit too like it will emerge, because once a government has an instrument in its hand, it will be prompted to make more and more use of it by what it perceives as necessity and exigency; and in ways that the government which first introduced it promised, hand on heart, would never be allowed.

Another explanation – alas, far more likely – is that it is the usual rather unintelligent nostrum that someone invents or revives in trying to deal with a problem or set of problems faced at a given time. Thus, the idea of mandatory ID cards has been prompted by a variety of considerations including immigration, identity fraud, crime and terrorism. In accordance with these ambiguous aims the two Home Secretaries who have promoted an ID-card scheme have experimented with a number of different rationalisations for having them.

First there was talk of 'entitlement cards', aimed at making it impossible for illegal immigrants to get jobs or benefits because they would not have a card that everyone else in the legitimate population would have. As before, requiring the entire population to carry mandatory civil-liberties-reducing ID cards to stop an illegal immigrant from carrying bricks on a building site is like killing flies with atom bombs, but the devisers of the scheme do not see this because they are so fixated on the immigrant problem.

Then there was (briefly) talk of protection against terrorism, until it was pointed out that almost all the hijackers of the 9/11 aeroplanes had satisfactory ID and were legally in the United States.

Then the rationalisation turned to identity fraud, but this – as everyone always points out – is a matter for credit and store card companies and their clients, and for the personal responsibility of individuals to ensure that their bills and bank statements do not fall into criminal hands – just as they do with the security of their homes and motor vehicles. No mandatory ID scheme is needed, nor will it stop identity fraud; as mentioned earlier, the criminal industry of stealing and manufacturing identities will simply be given a boost.

Part II: Evidence

The most devastating indictment of the proposed ID-card scheme I have ever seen, or that anyone could need to see, is the book of evidence presented to the Home Affairs Committee of the House of Commons: *House of Commons Home Affairs Committee IDENTITY CARDS: Fourth Report of Session 2003–4, Volume II*. To read that volume is to see, as plain as day, the wrong-headedness, impracticality, and vast expense of the scheme mooted by the Home Office.

The volume should of course be read itself. It will be seen that the expert bodies best informed on matters of law, human rights and civil liberties are unanimous in their opposition to it: the Law Society, Liberty (the civil liberties NGO), Justice (a distinguished all-party law and human rights organisation), Privacy International (the human rights group that monitors technological implications for civil liberties, and provides assessments of public policy on surveillance and analogous activities of corporations), and others, even among them the Information Commissioner, criticise the proposals. The British Medical Association expressed its disquiet over the idea of having to have ID-card readers in hospitals to determine whether a patient is eligible for treatment, the Commission for Racial Equality expressed concerns over the use of ID-card vetting by police – in short, from every quarter there were considered and conclusive objections to ID cards. Very little of this is evident in the Committee's eventual report, which is a grave cause for concern, because the insistence of the Home Office in continuing with proposals for legislation in the face of such a countervailing weight shows that it is determined to ignore it.

It is sufficient to cite just some of the 'Supplementary memorandum' submitted by the all-party organisation Justice. After iterating its view, first given in earlier debates on ID cards, that they represent 'a major invasion of individual privacy', Justice points out that the logistical undertaking involved is almost insuperable. In some London boroughs the annual turnover of addresses exceeds 60 per cent, which means that tens of thousands of people would have to update their ID cards every year. The unreliability of even the most sophisticated technology in recording biometric data would result in thousands of people being inconvenienced either by being unable to get cards at all (their irises not being suitable for recording, or having no hands from which fingerprints can be taken, or being intersexed and having no identifiable gender), while the government itself recognises that almost one in every six people 'fail biometric tests set at the highest level of corroboration'.

The cost of recording the biometric data of those who are recordable, the cost of card readers in hospitals, benefit offices and elsewhere, the constantly rising price of cards to people whose data have changed (they have moved house) or have lost cards or had them stolen, the problems of people temporarily cardless for one or other of these reasons, or who have not updated their cards – all these paint a nightmare scenario of expense and inconvenience which is not only profoundly problematic in itself but – in light of the ineffectiveness of ID cards for any of the purposes the government cites for them – absurd. 'ID cards seem unlikely to meet many of the alleged needs for which they are being introduced,' Justice continues. 'The Home Secretary acknowledged before the Committee that their use against terrorism is limited. So, too, would be their use against illegal immigration. It is difficult to see that the position of illegal Chinese workers discovered in Morecambe would have been any different if an ID register had been in effect. Spain found its ID cards useless in preventing the outrage in Madrid. ... ID may inhibit – but will undoubtedly not eliminate – identity fraud and they should limit entitlement to public services. It seems unlikely that, by reference to these objectives alone, they will be cost effective.'

Justice was not alone in concluding that the ID-card scheme will prove an enormously costly white elephant. None of those who submitted evidence took into account the fact that, as the implications of the scheme become better known, both as to cost and as to invasion of privacy and curtailment of liberty, non-compliance with it will increase. The hope that the voluntary phase of the scheme would result in an 80 per cent take-up is premised on the increasing inconvenience to individuals of not having a card. Nicola Roche, the official serving as Director of the Identity Cards project in the Home Office, said of the envisaged compulsory phase, 'For those who do not have a card, life would be very uncomfortable in that phase because what the Government has said is that they would want access to free public services accessed through an identity card. So if you did not have one, life would become very difficult. We would also expect that a range of private sector services would also use the card.' That this was the hope too for the voluntary phase is shown by her saying that in the voluntary phase 'life [would be] increasingly difficult' without an ID card.

The first pages of the volume of evidence are devoted to the testimony given by Home Office officials to the enquiry. One's heart goes out to the officials, required to serve as advocates for a scheme it is obvious they do not themselves endorse. This becomes increasingly evident as puzzled MPs quiz them on how the scheme would be implemented. The government proposes to begin with a voluntary ID scheme, eventually becoming mandatory for all. It is not clear why they choose to proceed in this way, unless they are hoping that familiarity will make ID cards more acceptable and useful over time (by making lack of them uncomfortable), plus spreading the burden of cost and distribution. A magic figure has been plucked out of the air that 80 per cent of people will avail themselves of voluntary ID cards before whatever government is in power in about 2013 moves to a mandatory system.

But the ill-thought-out nature of the scheme, and the government's concealment of the likely true cost, is made very clear by the evasive answers given by Mr Stephen Harrison to questions from David Winnick MP and the Committee's Chairman on the cost.

Winnick: What at the end of the day would be the total estimated cost?

Harrison: I think in terms of looking at that, forgive me for trying to give you a sort of lengthier answer on this, I think it depends at what point one draws the line because in a sense the scheme ...

Winnick: What would be the round figure? Is that difficult to answer?

Harrison: What is the end of the day in that sense? Even if you reach a point ...

Chairman: Mr Harrison, in the Government's consultation document last year you published a figure of £3,145 million.

Harrison: Yes.

Chairman: Is that still your estimate?

Harrison: There was actually a range of figures which were published and what that was based on was adding costs and we talk about the period at which you cut off. That was based ...

Chairman: Is that our best figure?

Harrison: We have better estimates of some of the detailed costs that have gone on.

Winnick: You seem to be rather evasive about this ...

Harrison: On the consultation paper there was a range of costs and it varied from 1.3 billion to 3.1 billion ...[x]

This classic encounter has been long superseded by government admissions that the cost would be in the region of £5.5 billion at least, and as we saw earlier that estimate is regarded by all informed opinion as far too low. Even at £5 billion – a cost to be borne by every individual aged sixteen and over in the United Kingdom – a scheme that is of very doubtful usefulness, which is far from being guaranteed actually to work, and yet which drastically undercuts civil liberties, seems to be not just an exceptionally poor bargain, but a downright foolish one.

In its own document submitted to the Committee, the Home Office makes a number of claims which do not stand up under scrutiny. For example, it points to the fact that most other EU countries have ID cards as a justification for the introduction of an ID-card scheme in the UK. It does not mention that none of these schemes is linked to a central National Identity Register, or involves the coding of biometric data onto a chip. Nor do they mention that the schemes in those countries are very inexpensive, and do not by themselves suffice to establish full identity for such purposes as opening bank accounts or securing mortgages.

The Home Office reports public acceptability of the idea of ID cards, having conducted some polling and focus group studies; it does not point out that polling also shows a high level of resistance to having to pay for cards, nor the fact that those opposed to the cards – a substantial enough number of whom might refuse to get ID cards to make the scheme overall unworkable – are well informed and sterling in their opposition. Its own evidence to the Committee makes astonishingly tentative claims: they are that ID cards will make controls on illegal immigrants 'more effective', will make checks 'more reliable', will make employers' compliance with checks on illegals 'easier', that is, far from any guarantee of solving the problems at stake, they will (it is hoped by the Home Office) offer an improvement in policing them. Again, a very costly national

ID-card scheme seems a high price to pay for such modest benefits, even if they accrue.

No

It would be a triumph for liberty and good sense if the growing campaign against the ID-card scheme were to result in the Home Office abandoning its proposals, consigning them to the same political limbo where periodic attempts to revive the death penalty and other illiberal nostrums reside. The ID-card debate has been held before, and ID-card schemes have been rejected before.

The world is not a different place from what it was when those debates were held; the specious argument that 9/11 has changed everything is false. 9/11 was a tragedy and a shock; and the civilised world was outraged by it; but a sense of proportion demands that we remember that during the Second World War the death and destruction seen on 9/11 was repeated and usually exceeded almost every night for years in the cities of Europe – in the Blitz and the Allied bombing campaigns – and in that terrible emergency the most that the British people allowed themselves was *temporary* suspension of liberties and a *temporary* ID-card scheme.

As to the arguments about illegal immigration and crime: if it is really true that only an expensive and all-embracing ID-card scheme can do no more than 'do more', then this is an admission of failure on the part of the authorities to deal with these problems now, consistently with the liberties and privacy of the population at large. Since the ID-card nostrum is not guaranteed success – rather, the opposite – but at immense cost, this effort at dealing with the problem is highly questionable.

Our government seeks to protect us from crime, terror and illegal immigration by restricting our liberties, and creating expensive new inconveniences. That is a very bad exchange, and an unnecessary and short-sighted admission of defeat. Let us hope and pray that better sense will prevail, and that the ID-card scheme proposals will eventually be rejected by our Parliamentarians and the public at large.

i   The relevant documents are House of Commons Home Affairs Committee 'Identity Cards' Fourth Report of the Session 2003–4, Volumes I and II.

ii   John Milton, *Defensio secunda*, 1638.

iii   The more so when one considers ID card fraud: look at what one can buy in the way of extremely plausible EU ID cards even today on the website of 'Phatism ID', http://www.phatism.com/fake-id-uk.

iv   David Blunkett interviewed on BBC. Sunday, 21 September, 2003.

v   Exigencies meant that rationing and other wartime inconveniences persisted for several years after the war's end, in the midst of a major reforming enterprise and in economic conditions of emergency. ID cards themselves were abolished in 1952.

vi   E. M. Forster, 'Liberty in England', *Abinger Harvest*, London, 1936, pp. 64–5.

vii   Roy Jenkins, *The Labour Case*, Penguin Special, 1959, p.135.

viii   Ibid.

ix   Ibid., p.137.

x   House of Commons Home Affairs Committee 'Identity Cards' Fourth Report of the Session 2003–4, Volume II, p. 10.